The Russians in Focus

RUSSIANS
IN FOCUS

by Harold J. Berman

Essay Index Reprint Series

 BOOKS FOR LIBRARIES PRESS
FREEPORT, NEW YORK

STANDARD BOOK NUMBER:

8369-1391-4

LIBRARY OF CONGRESS CATALOG CARD NUMBER:

71-90610

PRINTED IN THE UNITED STATES OF AMERICA

TO RUTH

Acknowledgments

THE author wishes to thank the *Atlantic Monthly* for permission to reprint and revise chapters which originally appeared in its pages.

The chapter on "Soviet Medical Care" is based in large part on material gathered by Mark C. Field, whose co-operation is herewith gratefully acknowledged. Mr. Field, a graduate student fellow of the Russian Research Center of Harvard University, is the author of a forthcoming Ph.D. thesis on the role of the doctor in Soviet society.

The chapter on "The Soviet Press" is based primarily on material presented in Alex Inkeles's chapters on the press in his book *Public Opinion in the Soviet Union* (Harvard University Press, 1950), and in two articles by Alex Inkeles and Kent Geiger entitled "Critical Letters to the Editors of the Soviet

Press," to be published in the *American Sociological Review*. I thank the authors for their permission to draw on their work. They are of course in no way responsible for my views and conclusions.

The collaboration of Miroslav Kerner in gathering material for the chapter on "The Soviet Soldier," and of Boris Konstantinovsky in recounting experiences which form the basis of the chapter on "Soviet Law in Action," is also gratefully acknowledged. The subject matter of the former chapter is more fully developed in a forthcoming book: Berman and Kerner, *Soviet Military Law*. The latter chapter is drawn, with the permission of the Harvard University Press, from the recent book: Berman and Konstantinovsky, *Soviet Law in Action*.

H. J. B.

Foreword

EDWARD Crankshaw, the noted English writer on Soviet affairs, complained a few years ago that Americans have a "total lack of objective curiosity" about the Russians and that the only question they ask him is, "When shall we have to fight them?" If he is right, this book is largely wasted effort. Its purpose is to give honest answers to honest questions about some of the basic facts of Soviet life. It is a product of the author's belief that there are many Americans who have a good deal of "objective curiosity" about the Russians, and that it is the responsibility of scholars in the field of Soviet studies to help them both to satisfy and to develop that curiosity.

There have been some penetrating interpretations of Russian society — of the more recent, perhaps the best is Sir John Maynard's *Russia in Flux;* another good one is Crankshaw's *Russia and the Russians.* Also there have been many excellent works on particular aspects of the Soviet social order — its economy, its governmental structure, its army, and so forth. There remains a need, however, for a short, concise statement of some of the basic characteristics of everyday Soviet life, a close-up of the Soviet system, presenting in a simple and understandable way elementary truths about the situation of the Russian people. This book seeks to meet that need. It makes no pretense of completeness, but presents what the author believes to be a basic minimum that any educated American should know in order to form judgments about the Soviet way of life.

Whatever judgments we form must be based on either misunderstanding or on understanding. But for Americans to understand a society so different from our own as the Soviet, requires a kind of thinking which we are not used to. From the eighteenth and nineteenth centuries we have inherited a kind of mechanistic thinking, which sees things in terms of black or white, good or evil, yes or no. In the twentieth century there has developed a kind of skepticism which sees things as gray, amoral, indifferent. But Soviet Russia is full of paradoxes — as is America, in fact, but we have grown up in America and tend to accept its paradoxical qualities unquestioningly. The name Soviet Russia is in itself partly a contradiction in terms: is it Soviet or is it Russian? It is both; it is full of blacks *and* whites, goods *and* evils, yeses *and* noes. In each of the following chapters I have tried to give full play to the contradictions and, at the same time, to suggest, at least, some explanations.

One more introductory word: In the interest of making a short readable book, I have omitted almost entirely footnote references to the sources of my information. I have relied upon Soviet textbooks and treatises, journals, newspapers, legislation, reports of court cases, and other official sources — from which a wealth of reliable information can be extracted if one is careful — and upon my knowledge of the Russian people gained especially in Europe, during and after the war. In many places I have reported recollected experiences of former Soviet citizens. I shall be happy to give any reader — or reviewer — the sources of my information with respect to any of the facts presented.

HAROLD J. BERMAN

Contents

The Russians in Focus

1

The Soviet Soldier

EACH YEAR between September 15th and October 15th, some million-and-one-half citizens of the Soviet Union, whose nineteenth birthday falls in the current year or who have completed their secondary education, are conscripted into the armed forces. Most of them serve as privates in the ground forces for the next two years; those who become noncommissioned officers in the ground forces serve for three years; if assigned to the air force, they may expect four years of service; if to the navy, five. Upon discharge they are placed in the reserve and are called up periodically for one to three months of training until they are fifty.

If we compare the rigors of Soviet military life, even in time of peace, with the comforts of American civilian life, or even with the deprivations of

American peacetime military service, we must wonder at the apparent equanimity and even, in some
cases, eagerness, with which these Soviet youths un-
dertake their new duties. But of course they do not
make the same comparison.

The new Soviet recruits have been prepared for
military discipline by their nineteen years' experience of a mobilized social order. They are accustomed to restrictions upon travel, fines for lateness
to work and absenteeism, two to four months' imprisonment for quitting a job without authorization. Many of them were drafted at the age of
fourteen for the State Labor Reserves, sent to
training schools for three years and then assigned
to factories. In respect to food and even to housing,
many will find the army a distinct improvement
over civilian life. Most of them come from collective farms and are excited by the prospect of
seeing new people and new places. Many will learn
new jobs, which will be useful upon return to
civilian life.

Above all, these nineteen-year-olds have been
brought up in a revolution which has deliberately

applied to peacetime pursuits a war philosophy — that is, a philosophy of discipline, self-sacrifice, unity, collective action, central planning (in earlier days Soviet leaders likened the State Planning Commission to the German General Staff). The Soviet recruit is accustomed, even at his age, to being recruited. All his life he has seen or heard or read about shock brigades on the collective farm front, Heroes of Socialist Labor, and many others who in their daily pursuits "storm bastions" of one kind or another.

In addition, and more particularly, the new Soviet conscript has previously undergone several hundred hours of military training in school, starting in the seventh grade. If at the age of fourteen or thereafter he joined the sixteen million members of the voluntary civil defense organization (now called Dosaav), he has also received extensive pre-military training in such skills as first aid, rifle marksmanship, the use of submachine guns and mortars, and parachute jumping, and has perhaps belonged to a radio club, ski club, club for training dogs for the service, or some other Dosaav unit.

Still, though he knows what to expect, he has very probably never before been subjected to so high a degree of sustained regimentation. The Soviet soldier undergoes strenuous training ten hours a day, six days a week. Furloughs are usually granted only in case of emergency. Together with his physical and technical labors, he is subjected to a most rigid discipline, including many hours — reportedly sixteen hours a week — of political indoctrination and education.

It was the original Bolshevik theory that the discipline of the Red Army should be based principally on a spirit of revolutionary zeal and camaraderie. From 1918 to 1939 the Soviet soldier, upon entering the army, took an oath "before the toiling classes of Russia and the whole world" pledging himself "to direct my every action and thought toward the liberation of all workers." All decorations, insignia, and ranks were eliminated, and titles (company commander, regimental commander, and so forth) were based on the job done. Saluting was abolished, and all personnel addressed each other as "comrade."

From the mid-1930's on, there has been a continuing revival of prerevolutionary Russian military traditions and a shift of emphasis away from class-consciousness toward Soviet patriotism and discipline for its own sake. In 1935 the traditional ranks of lieutenant, captain, colonel, and the like, were restored. In 1940 the rank of general was reintroduced. Also in 1940 the duty to salute was imposed. (Soviet noncommissioned officers must also be saluted by their inferiors, and a failure to salute may bring several days of K.P.) In 1943 the title "officer" was restored, together with the traditional Russian officers' insignia of rank, the gold braid epaulets. In 1946 the names Red Army and Red Fleet were replaced by Soviet Army and Soviet Fleet.

The new military oath, introduced in 1939, abandons the old revolutionary phraseology and stresses the qualities of a good soldier as such. The Soviet soldier now pledges himself "to be an honest, courageous, disciplined and alert soldier," and "to defend the motherland bravely, skillfully, with dignity and honor, sparing neither my blood nor my life itself to gain complete victory over the enemy." Containing almost two hundred words, the oath must be learned by heart by all Soviet troops. It is considered a basic document of military discipline and military law.

In 1940, after the Finnish war, a new Disciplinary Code was enacted, whose severity was typified by the imposition of an absolute duty of obedience, the superior having "the right to take all measures of coercion, including the application of force and arms" in order to compel such obedience. In 1946 a more lenient Disciplinary Code was enacted, which restricted the superior's right of coercion to cases "of utmost urgency," and which omitted the earlier provision that the superior "shall not be liable for the consequences."

The disciplinary powers of both noncommissioned and commissioned officers are very wide. Confinement in the guardhouse up to twenty days, and reduction in military rank, may in proper cases be imposed on enlisted men and officers, by their superiors, without benefit of court-martial. Oral reprimand before assembled troops is apparently a common form of company punishment, and extends even to generals and admirals, who may be reprimanded before an assembly of officers.

On the other hand, the Soviet system of military discipline also stresses rewards for exemplary conduct, including valuable gifts, money, and, characteristically, a personal photograph in front of the unfurled unit banner.

More serious offenses against military order and discipline are subject to criminal trial by military tribunals and, in general, to heavier punishment. Departure without leave with intent to be absent up to two hours, if it is the second offense, or from two to twenty-four hours, first offense, is punishable in time of peace by sentence to a disciplinary battalion from six months to two years; departure without leave with intent to be absent for more than twenty-four hours is considered to be desertion and is punishable in time of peace by deprivation of freedom (that is, sentence to a labor camp) from five to ten years.

Usually the factors of intent and motive play an

important part in Soviet criminal law; however, there are some glaring exceptions. The Criminal Code provides that if a serviceman deserts and flees across the frontier, adult members of his family may be exiled to remote regions of Siberia for five years — even though they had no part whatsoever in his crime.

On the whole, however, the Soviet system of military courts and procedure seems to afford the serviceman a fair trial, at least in time of peace. The courts are permanent courts, independent of the commanders, with professional judges and prosecutors. Appeals may go up to the Supreme Court of the U.S.S.R., which has a military division, and many Supreme Court cases involving crimes by servicemen are reported. However, it should be noted that the elaborate and time-consuming process of trial in the military courts is complemented by the wide powers of informal nonjudicial punishment for disciplinary offenses; a commanding officer may himself mete out quite severe punishment to a subordinate and thus avoid the risk of his acquittal by a military tribunal. The subordinate, however, may complain against such punishment to the commander's superior officer.

Soviet military discipline is explicitly based on inequalities of rank and privilege. "Equality-mongering," denounced by Stalin as a "left deviation," is considered to be dangerous to the maintenance of order; also it is considered a threat to ambition and initiative. In the army this philosophy is carried to such an extreme that sergeants receive almost five times as much pay as privates, colonels receive almost twice as much as captains, and generals from one-and-a-half to two-and-a-half times as much as colonels.

As important as pay differentials, are the extra privileges that go with higher rank. The officer is far better dressed, and has special commissary privileges; if he is of field grade he has a personal servant.

One interesting symbol of the emphasis on distinctions of rank is the restoration, by the 1946 Disciplinary Code, of the prerevolutionary institution of Officers' Courts of Honor. In these courts, officers are tried by their fellows for "offenses unworthy of the rank of officer which infringe mili-

tary honor or are not compatible with moral rules."
If the court finds the officer guilty, it may issue a
warning or a reprimand or may recommend demo-
tion or transfer. All that now seems to be missing is
the prerevolutionary institution of the duel; although it was widely rumored a few years ago that
two famous Soviet generals were only dissuaded
from a duel by the personal intervention of Stalin.

Generally speaking, careers are open to talent in
the Soviet armed forces. Training courses are available to qualified privates who wish to become noncommissioned officers; officer candidate schools are
also open to those who qualify. One step in the op-
posite direction has been taken, however: Suvorov
Schools, named after the famous eighteenth-century
Russian general, and Nakhimov Schools, named
after a famous Russian admiral, were established in
1943 to prepare children from the age of nine for
officer candidate schools; in admission to these
schools, priority is given to the sons of officers as
well as to certain other groups.

The Soviet officer does not get his extra pay and
his privileges for nothing. Like all Soviet officials,

he is under strict surveillance and is punishable for "abuse of authority" and for "a negligent attitude toward service duties." The commander of a supply depot who distributes supplies without observing the required formalities, or the commander of a military institution who expends for current requirements funds assigned for money reserves, counting on receiving in time assignments to cover the expenditures, is liable to imprisonment for not less than six months. Moreover, the 1940 Disciplinary Code stated flatly that the commander is responsible for the acts of his subordinates, and although this provision was omitted in the 1946 Code it still reflects current practice in many cases.

Officers are under surveillance particularly by the Communist Party organs within the army and by the secret informers of the Ministry of State Security.

Since the 1942 statute abolishing the office of military commissar and introducing "strict one-man control" in the armed forces, the work of the Communist Party organs has been directed chiefly to propaganda among the soldiers, discipline and, in general, what we would call morale. The Chief Political Administrations of the various military units, representing the Party, not only conduct formal political education (through lectures, seminars, group and individual discussions, and other media) but also provide libraries, cinema and theater facilities, concerts, newspapers, and a wide variety of entertainment.

Theoretically, at least, the commanding officer of a unit is solely responsible for the military activities of the unit. However, the line between the political and the military is not easy to maintain. As a recent Soviet writer, Major General D. Ortenberg, has stated: "There is not a single part of the unit's life upon which the political organs do not exert their influence. Military training and political education are inseparably connected in our army."

However much the Party may be a thorn in the side of the commanding officers, and however much its heavy indoctrination may prevent any expression of political dissent whether by officers or men, nevertheless the Party also serves to channel the grievances of the men to higher authorities.

This is also true of the secret informers of the Special Sections of the Ministry of State Security.

The job of the Special Sections is to report on anti-Soviet activities in the army, but they also check on administrative and other matters. A Soviet D.P. who has a wide first-hand knowledge of Soviet military life recounts the following episode:

A commander of a rank regiment of the Byelorussian Military District was summoned to the Special Section of the corps. "The devil knows what's going on in your kitchen," the head of the Special Section said. The regiment commander replied that as far as he knew there were no special irregularities. "How come, then," he was asked, "that you find it all right if the soup bucket is stopped up with a rag? And why didn't you report that the quartermaster company of your regiment attempted collectively to refuse to participate in the daily routine?"

Finally dismissed by the head of the Special Section, with instructions to investigate and report on these matters, the regiment commander returned to his unit, and upon inquiry discovered that the previous night a tiny hole had been found in the soup bucket and had been temporarily stopped up with a rag, and further that at the time of assembly for the daily routine two or three soldiers had remarked, in view of a heavy downpour of rain, "How nice it would be if there were no routine today." An overzealous informer had blown these items up into a secret report of inefficiency and rebelliousness.

Another story, this one taken from an official report of a wartime case in the Supreme Court of the U.S.S.R., also casts ironic light on the way in which political and military matters may overlap in the life of the Soviet soldier. The case involved an army sergeant who was court-martialed for having "systematically uttered anti-Soviet opinions." It seems that the sergeant, whose military and political record was otherwise unassailable, had, in performing his military duties, expressed certain unfavorable opinions regarding the Constitution of the U.S.S.R. In sustaining an acquittal the Supreme Court stated:

"Although these opinions were often clothed in rough unworthy form and contain politically incorrect formulations, however . . . it is clear that all these opinions were directed toward the strengthening of military discipline." It appeared from the evidence, the court said, that the accused "was a demanding person in connection with discipline."

Apparently someone provoked the sergeant by relying on his Constitutional rights. Very likely the deputy regiment commander for political affairs pressed charges. Whether in peacetime the sergeant would have fared so well in the courts is open to question.

2

The Soviet Peasant

ALTHOUGH some twenty million Soviet citizens moved from the country to the city between 1929 and 1939, as part of the government's program of rapid industrialization, Russia is still predominantly an agricultural country. Only about one third of its two hundred million people live in cities. Over half live by farming, forestry, and fishing. The fifth Five-Year Plan adopted in 1952, in contrast to previous Five-Year Plans, anticipates no appreciable change in these proportions.

Moreover, most of the city dwellers have close connections with peasant life. A very large proportion of them have themselves worked as peasants; many still go back to the villages to help with the harvest; many cultivate vegetable plots and raise poultry and livestock in their free time.

Peasant life in Russia, as elsewhere, is notoriously conservative. Relying on nature, the peasant is accustomed to a slow rhythm of both thought and action. He is also mentally and physically less accessible than his urban brother to governmental pressures. Only by what Stalin himself called "a second revolution," "a revolution from above," did the Bolshevik regime succeed in uprooting the traditions of the Russian peasantry and creating a new form of agricultural economy: the collective farm.

Between 1929 and 1932, some twenty million small peasant landholdings were consolidated into about 240,000 collective farms. In theory the new collective farms were voluntary associations of farmers, who pooled their resources to form a large co-operative enterprise; in fact, they were formed by compulsion exerted chiefly by the Communist Party, against the tremendous resistance of the peasants, hundreds of thousands of whom were sent to labor camps. The results were: violence, illegal slaughter of horses and other livestock, illegal disposal of crops, graft, waste, refusal to work — and famine. In 1944 Stalin told Churchill that the suffering of the collectivization period surpassed even that of World War II.

Peasant resistance was not in vain. Writing of the peasant's role in Russian history, Sir John Maynard states: "He is no strategist and lacks the qualities of leadership: but he has shown more than once that he can say No with conclusive emphasis." The peasant's No did not force the Soviet state to abandon the collectivization program, but it did cause it to make important modifications of the original objectives of that program.

The original idea of collectivization was the ultimate conversion of the entire peasantry into a rural proletariat, working for wages on giant state-owned "factories in the fields." By 1935 this idea was largely spent, although some "state" farms, on which peasants work for wages, were organized and continue to exist. The chief concessions won by 97 per cent of the peasants on the "collective" farms were: first, the right to keep for themselves what remained after heavy government taxes in kind, and second, the right of each peasant household to maintain its own house-and-garden plot. These conces-

sions have not deprived the government of what, from its point of view, is perhaps the chief benefit of collectivization: the ability to collect what it wants from the farms for delivery to the cities. Further, the state controls the collective farms through about 7000 machine-tractor stations, which furnish both machinery and operators, and which have made Soviet agriculture almost as highly mechanized as that of the United States. The MTS (machine-tractor station) charges very dearly for its services, not in money but in kind.

The Soviet peasant continues to pay a very high price, in poverty and regimentation, for Russia's industrialization. Nevertheless, he has kept his identity and his individualism to a surprising extent.

The individual peasant on a Soviet collective farm is not paid wages, strictly speaking, but he receives a share of the profits of the collective — his share being calculated on the basis of what he has produced. Shares are measured in terms of so-called "labor days." Under a law of 1948 there are nine different labor-day rates, ranging from half a labor day for the least skilled work to two-and-one-

half labor days for the most skilled and most difficult. A worker who weeds an acre of onions may
be credited with half a labor day, while a worker
who picks two acres of cotton may receive two-
and-one-half labor days.

A labor day is only a percentage share of the
total income of the collective farm. At the end of
the fiscal year, each collective divides its total net
product (after taxes and reserves) by the total number of labor days earned by the members. The
larger the product, the greater the value of a labor
day — and the richer the peasants of the particular
collective farm. Inequalities of net income of different collective farms may be considerable, though
they are somewhat lessened by taxation, which is
based on potential production, determined according to total arable acreage. Soviet literature refers
proudly to "millionnaire collective farms."

As in the factory, piece-rate payments are part
of a larger system of incentives. Orders, medals,
titles, and bonuses are given to peasants who exceed the indices established for production of different crops, for breeding of cattle, for milking,

and for other tasks. The peasants work chiefly in brigades consisting usually of thirty to sixty members, each brigade cultivating a certain area for one or several seasons; bonuses consisting of a percentage of beyond-plan production are paid to individual brigades and to individual squads within a brigade.

A sense of "socialist competition" is encouraged by special rewards for breaking of records. "Shock brigadiers" and "model workers" are given trips to Moscow, get their pictures in the papers, and are hailed at public meetings. The more promising and industrious are given the opportunity to study to become agronomists, teachers, engineers, doctors.

The specialization of work on the collective farm may also provide satisfactions. It is said that the Soviet collective farmer is more than just a peasant: he is a dairy worker, or tractor driver, or watchman, or squad leader, or brigadier, or bookkeeper, or even manager. Such designations are said to have special appeal to peasant women, who now comprise a sizable majority of the peasant working population, and whose position before the revolution was one of marked inferiority. Today the equality of peasant women is, in general, protected. They do not have to turn over their pay to their husbands. They may rise to positions of leadership, though relatively few are collective farm chairmen. However, they probably comprise 70 per cent of all squad leaders.

Again as in the factory, rewards for success are matched by punishments for failure. For disciplinary violations, such as failure to report to work without adequate reason, or refusal to obey orders, peasants may be warned, reprimanded, rebuked at the general meeting of the collective farm; they may have their names placed on a blackboard; they may be fined up to five labor days, demoted, suspended, or even expelled.

In contrast to the industrial enterprise, which both in theory and in practice is run by the manager (under strict state and Party controls, to be sure), the collective farm is in theory — though not in practice — run by the general membership meeting. It is not easy to understand why the fiction is maintained that the general meeting elects and controls the collective farm chairman, when — as the Soviet press and even Soviet legislatures periodically complain — the chairman is sent in from the outside, and has complete power over the collective.

The official complaints against undemocratic practices in internal collective farm government may reflect the difficulties of Party control of collective farm chairmen once they are appointed. Perhaps, in Aesopian style, the real complaint is that the general meetings have too much power! There is a very heavy turnover of chairmen. Also there is a very complex system of controls over a particular collective farm: its production quotas are assigned by the Ministry of Agriculture, its work methods are to an important degree controlled by the machine-tractor station, its deliveries to the state and its general operations are supervised by local and district government organs. There are, of course, Communist Party agencies standing behind each of these state and economic bodies and, at the same time, the Party has its own agricultural organization. There have been official complaints that

Party agencies have tried to displace the local offices of the Ministry of Agriculture.

The collective farms are under almost continual fire for so-called bureaucratism. A statute of September 1946 inveighed against "the undue increase of executive and service personnel in the collective farms and the exceedingly high waste of labor days and money for the cost of administration . . . Grafters and parasites frequently hide themselves in useless, artificially invented jobs."

Similarly there have been complaints against the peasants' habit of underestimating their production in order to evade government collections. "In the Bashkir Autonomous Republic," one writer stated in 1946: "the state production quotas have not been met. The explanation given is shortage of fuel, which is untrue. It is not because of lack of fuel but because of the anti-government attitudes which exist in the region."

Difficulties of administrative and political control have been intensified by the smallness of the collective farms. In 1949 there were about 253,000, averaging about seventy-five families and about

1200 acres under cultivation. Only one out of three or four collective farms contained a Party organization. In the year 1950, through administrative mergers of the smaller collectives, the total number was reduced to 123,000, and by 1952 the number was down to about 97,000. In the Moscow region, for example, 6000 collective farms were consolidated into about 1700, averaging about 1800 acres and 250 able-bodied farmers apiece. In one province of the Ukraine, 866 collective farms were merged into 342, averaging 7400 acres each. It is now reported that a majority of collectives have their own Party organizations.

The drive to consolidate the collectives was accompanied by a revival of the controversy of the thirties regarding a "rural proletariat." A member of the Politburo, Khrushchev, advocated not only an administrative consolidation but a physical amalgamation of collectives, and the formation of "agro-towns" in which the peasants would live in apartment houses. To an outsider who knows something of Soviet means of transportation and Soviet peasant housing, the idea seems — and seemed — fantastic. It was propagated for some months, implemented in a few places, then criticized, then dropped like a hot potato.

While the administrative merger of collective farms does not seem to have altered seriously the pattern of peasant life established in the mid-1930's, the transfer of peasants to agro-towns would have deprived the Russian peasant of the one thing he cherishes most: the peasant household. In the early days of collectivization, Soviet radicals proclaimed that "the peasant household as a separate unit is doomed." In 1935 the recognition of the rights of the peasant household was perhaps the most important means of reconciling the peasantry to collectivization.

Centuries of Russian history are embodied in the institution of the Soviet peasant household. Originating in ancient times, it has survived many different forms of agricultural organization. Defined by the Soviet Land Code as "a family-labor association of persons jointly engaged in agriculture," it may consist of any number of persons (today it rarely exceeds fifteen), related by blood or by marriage or by adoption into the household, who carry on a joint domestic economy.

Under Soviet law, the land that may belong to a peasant household is restricted to an area between five eighths of an acre and two-and-one-half acres, depending on the type of collective farm. Peasant household land comprises only about 5 per cent of the total area under cultivation. Nevertheless, peasant household land in some years accounts for about 20 per cent of the total agricultural production.

Soviet law permits a peasant household to own one cow, two calves, one sow with sucklings, ten sheep and goats, an unlimited number of fowls and rabbits, and twenty beehives. In nomadic and semi-nomadic areas some other animals may also be owned. Despite these limitations, peasant households owned, before the war, about 65 per cent of the cows and calves in the Soviet Union, and over half the pigs and sheep; they provide a large proportion of Soviet meat, vegetables, fruits, poultry, dairy products, and honey.

The peasant would like to devote his energies as

much as possible to his household plot. In order to secure the deliveries which it desires, the government has passed laws requiring that a certain minimum amount of labor days be earned in the collective fields, and combating the illegal encroachment of households onto collective fields. Also the peasant households are taxed. Nevertheless, the income from their plots probably remains at least as large a source of income to the peasants as their income from the collectives.

The peasant takes the produce of his household plot, as well as his payments in kind for work on the collective fields, to the collective farm market. Here prices are free — and high, despite some competition from state food shops. There are said to be some 4500 such local free markets in the Soviet Union — over a thousand more than the total number of cities and towns. In 1939 they accounted for over 15 per cent of the total volume of trade, as measured in rubles. However, the peasants suffer from the shortage of consumers' goods, which they must buy in state-owned village shops or else at exorbitant prices in the free market; and the situation is aggravated by the decline in home industries such as weaving and shoemaking, which played a more important part before collectivization.

The members of the peasant household are bound by the closest ties. The rights of management, use, and disposal of all household property belong to the members as a whole; in the absence of unanimity, decisions are by majority vote of the adult members. The members select a head of the household to administer their affairs. The powers of the head are governed by tradition and custom. Occasionally cases get into the courts involving the rights of the peasant household — such as the right of the members not to have the head of the household sell a household building without their consent, or the right of a member to his share in the property of a household that has been dissolved, or the right of a household to recover damages from the "parent" collective farm for illegal withdrawal of the household plot.

At least as important as the economic and legal

aspects of the peasant household, however, is its social aspect as an institution for transmitting the tradition of peasant life from generation to generation. Soviet collectivization of agriculture has been superimposed on an older family collectivism. It is impossible to measure in quantitative terms the significance to Soviet society of the peasant way of life; it is equally impossible to doubt that its significance is tremendous.

A United Press correspondent in Russia in the late 1930's, desiring to write a feature story, journeyed one day from his Moscow hotel to a collective farm. On arrival there he found no one in the offices or in the fields. He was told that no one was working because it was Sunday. He had not known it was Sunday, because the Bolsheviks had changed the calendar, abolishing the seven-day week and instituting a five-day week, with rest days staggered for individual workers. He had known that it was four-day, fourteenth day of the month. The peasants, however, had kept their Day of Resurrection (as Sunday is called in Russian) — though it was on no official calendar.

In 1940 the Soviet government restored the traditional seven-day week with Sunday as a common day of rest. Undoubtedly Karl Marx would
count this as another example of what he called
"the idiocy of rural life."

3

The Soviet Worker

A BRITISH newspaper correspondent, recently returned from eighteen months in Moscow, describes the Soviet Union as "a tangle of paradoxes." "Whatever one's prejudices about the Soviet regime and the Russian people, for or against," he writes, "there are incontrovial facts to be found in Moscow to prove them to the hilt."

The extreme contradictions of Soviet life are nowhere more apparent than in the sphere of labor relations. By an appropriate selection of facts, one may draw a picture of the Soviet worker as a slave of the state and its bureaucracy, or as a protected and privileged member of the ruling class. It is easy to say that the truth lies somewhere in between — but that does not untangle the paradox.

The oppressive restraints upon the Soviet worker's freedom of movement are well known. Under legislation of 1940, still in force, a worker who is more than twenty minutes late for work is subject to a fine of 25 per cent of his monthly wages for six months; and a worker who leaves his job without the director's permission is subject to imprisonment for from two to four months. Labor books, in which dismissals, penalties, and other data are entered, are required to be kept for each worker. Social-insurance benefits depend partly upon length of continuous employment in the same enterprise.

Although there has been no general mobilization of labor, except during the war, the law permits compulsory transfer of engineers, technicians, bookkeepers, economists, and certain other specialists, as well as certain skilled workers. Also, roughly 700,-000 boys of fourteen and girls of fifteen are conscripted annually into the State Labor Reserves to be trained until they are seventeen (and in some cases up to nineteen), and then sent for several years to whatever job the authorities desire. In addition, there are the corrective-labor camps and labor colonies, in which convicts serve as a labor force for work projects of the Ministry of Internal Affairs.

To understand the reasons for the severe legal restrictions upon labor mobility, most of which have been introduced only since 1939, is also to understand the limits of their effectiveness. The scarcity of labor, and especially of skilled labor, in view of the heavy production demands made upon factory directors by the state, has facilitated widespread evasion of some of the restrictive laws.

The Soviet press still complains about malingering, absenteeism and heavy labor turnover. Labor books are easily lost; recruiting offices of plants in need of workers do not ask too many questions and find ways of circumventing the law. Furthermore, the law prohibits lateness, absenteeism, or unauthorized quitting, only when committed "without adequate reason." In interpreting this phrase, the courts have accepted medical and other excuses. The Supreme Court of the U.S.S.R. has sustained the right of a mother to quit her job, even without the director's permission, in order to take care of her sick children.

In the case of a worker who had served his four

months' imprisonment for unauthorized quitting, and who still refused to go back to his old job, Soviet courts have held that the labor contract was dissolved by the worker's earlier departure, even though it was unlawful, and that therefore he did not have to return. Thus the Soviet worker, in struggling against the bonds of immobility, may receive help from the manager, the doctor, and the lawyer. In addition, if he is admitted to a training course to improve his qualifications, the manager may not withhold permission to leave.

On balance, however, even apart from the new graduates of the State Labor Reserves and the inmates of the labor camps, Soviet workers can hardly be called free by American standards. "In the U.S.S.R. work is a duty and a matter of honor for every able-bodied citizen," states Article 12 of the Soviet Constitution, and, under Article 130, ". . . it is the duty of every citizen . . . to maintain labor discipline." These Constitutional duties, implemented by specific criminal laws, make the Soviet worker more like a soldier, or, as the Soviets say, "a fighter on the labor front."

On the other hand, the Soviet worker has considerable freedom to improve his condition by his own effort and ability. Here, too, the Constitution offers a guiding slogan: "The principle applied in the U.S.S.R. is that of socialism: 'From each according to his ability, to each according to his work.'" How literally and thoroughly this "socialist" principle is carried out may be judged by the existence of a nation-wide system of differentiated progressive scales of piece rates, with bonuses for extra efficiency for individual branches of industry and individual categories of workers. Thus the average wage for coal miners is about two-and-one-half times the average wage for workers generally; some coal miners — so-called "shock workers" and "Stakhanovites" — may earn as much as thirty times the general average. "Especially valuable specialists and practitioners" may receive "personal salaries" of an arbitrary amount outside any scale.

"Heroes of Socialist Labor" and holders of prizes such as the Order of Lenin receive special financial benefits. Workers' inventions and suggestions for improving production methods are rewarded generously. Extra profits of enterprises provide sources of bonuses and increased wages.

The extent to which the Soviet system encourages so-called "socialist competition" among workers is illustrated by a 1947 decree on the wages and salaries of personnel in stores and shops. Cashiers, bookkeepers, janitors, and other persons not directly connected with selling, receive fixed wages ranging from 175 to 560 rubles per month; in addition, if they work in the store or shop, they receive 1 per cent of their monthly wages for each per cent of profit made by the enterprise.

The manager of the store is paid on a percentage basis of .10 to .23 per cent of the turnover. Salesmen are also paid bonuses on a percentage basis of their actual sales — 5.1 per cent for toys and books; .4 per cent for shoes; .3 per cent for clothes; 2.6 per cent for perfumes and toilet articles; 1.4 per cent for other goods.

The emphasis upon rugged individualism among workers, in a country which has accomplished large-scale industrialization under state planning rather than under private enterprise, has created a labor aristocracy of the strong and skillful. Despite the shortage of consumers' goods, the labor aristocrat has a distinct advantage over his brother proletarian, for rent does not generally exceed 5 per cent of the monthly wage, and food is relatively cheap, so that a large money income makes it possible to purchase the better grades of clothing and some luxury goods.

Apart from liberty and equality, there is the question of fraternity. So acute an observer as Sir John Maynard has spoken of the " 'we'-feeling" in the Soviet factory, and the "sense of ownness" among the workers. Others have said that Soviet factories "belong" to the workers. Here, too, there are paradoxes to be untangled. Neither in political theory nor in law can the Soviet workers be said to own the factories. In modern Soviet theory, the state is identified with the entire Soviet people — the so-called "toilers," including "workers, peasants and intelligentsia" — so that it would be just as true to say that the peasants or the managers own the factories. And in Soviet law, the workers have, as regards the factory, none of the rights of possession, use or disposition which are associated with owner-ship.

Management of a Soviet factory is legally the monopoly of the factory director. In actual practice the triangle of director, secretary of the factory's Party organization, and chairman of the union factory committee, which was officially in control in the early 'thirties, has continued to exist informally in many plants. However, although the director is subject to controls from above, it is entirely within his discretion whether or not to consult with anyone else in the enterprise.

The trade union cannot lawfully interfere in the hiring of labor, in planning production or expansion, or in determining contractual relations with supplier or purchaser enterprises. In regard to dismissals, job classification, transfers of workers, and payment of wages, the union has no direct voice, but only an indirect one through the system of arbitration of grievances.

The Soviet trade union is a state organization. Its main job is the administration of social insurance and of workers' welfare generally, and the exhorta-

tion of the workers to increase productivity. Although strikes have occasionally occurred in the
Soviet Union, they have been wildcat strikes; should
any union leaders support a strike they would run
a grave risk of indictment for breach of labor discipline, if not for sabotage.

Nevertheless, it would be wrong to conclude that
the Soviet state identifies itself solely with management. Management, too, is a state organization under
severe limitations of independence and power. The
state imposes upon it important obligations toward
the workers. In the inevitable conflicts between
management and labor, the union plays an important role in protecting workers' rights. When
workers' grievances against management reach the
courts, as they often do, the workers are entitled to
the free services of a union lawyer, and the cases —
those officially reported as well as those recounted
by some former Soviet lawyers who have fled the
Soviet Union — show the Soviet courts to be, in
general, favorable to the workers.

For example, a worker who was fired sued for
reinstatement and back pay, on the ground that the

real reason for his dismissal was the fact that he had criticized the working conditions of the plant at union meetings and in the wall newspaper. (Enterprises are required to post informal newspapers to which workers may send comments and complaints.) The management argued that the worker was fired because he refused to be transferred to another plant of the same trust, and that the Labor Code permits dismissal on that ground. The court granted reinstatement, finding that the transfer was prompted by the management's desire to get rid of a man who had criticized it. It held that the provision of the Labor Code which permits dismissal for refusal to be transferred must be interpreted to refer only to transfers "in the interests of the business."

In other suits for reinstatement, management has defended itself on the ground that the worker was incompetent. The Labor Code gives management the right to dismiss a worker "in the event that he shows his unsuitability for the work." Although this provision might be interpreted as giving management full discretion to determine, in good faith, the

worker's unsuitability, the courts review the manager's decision and have often ordered reinstatement
on the ground that the worker was, in fact, compe-
tent.

These and other labor cases — involving job classification, vacation pay, severance pay, and similar
matters — do not come before the courts automatically, but are decided first in a grievance procedure
by an arbitration board consisting of equal numbers
of representatives of union and management. If the
union and management representatives fail to reach
an agreement, the worker may take the case to the
People's Court. Even if agreement is reached by
the arbitrators, their decision may be reviewed by
the People's Court if it is disapproved by a higher
union official called the Labor Inspector. In work-
men's-compensation cases involving injuries caused
by management's negligence, the worker may bring
court action against management for damages for
any loss of earning capacity beyond that which is
compensated by social insurance. Once in the courts,
the case may go all the way to the Supreme Court
of the U.S.S.R.

A striking feature of such litigation is the worker's protection against expense and delay. The worker who appears as a plaintiff in a labor case is exempt from the payment of court costs, and is entitled to the free services of the union lawyer. The court must hear the case not later than five days after commencement of the suit. A decision in favor of the worker is subject to immediate execution to the extent of a month's wages. If after the worker is paid, the favorable decision is reversed by a higher court, the sum paid (and indeed any sum mistakenly paid to a worker by management) may not be recovered from him, on the ground that "the limited budget of a worker should not be upset." Many former Soviet workers, now displaced persons, report that the union lawyer and the enterprise lawyer were considered the workers' friends, to whom they turned when in trouble.

It is in the interest of the Soviet state, of course, to foster a spirit of teamwork between management and labor. Managerial personnel of a state enterprise belong to the union local, and both the director and the union chairman are almost always members of the Communist Party. Moreover, the union is supposed to strive to increase the efficiency and productivity of the enterprise, while management is supposed to improve workers' housing (often supplied by the enterprise), health and safety conditions, and welfare in general.

However, too much teamwork may meet with disapproval from above. There have been complaints in the press that "in some factories businesslike relations [between management and union] are supplanted by domesticity and mutual backscratching." In the collective contract required to be drawn up annually in each enterprise, both sides are encouraged to make demands upon each other.

For example, in a typical collective contract signed in 1951 for the Moscow Food Combine "Mikoyan," the union promised a 3 per cent raise in efficiency, and management promised to mechanize the carrying of raw materials between certain departments, to repair the clubroom, and to improve dining facilities, especially for the night shifts.

Wages are not subject to bargaining; however, the pledges of management to introduce certain

machines, or to establish a certain number of "Sta-
khanov schools" for teaching workers methods of
increasing productivity, may in fact be a means of
raising wages, in view of the system of piece rates.

Although there is no legal enforcement of the
collective contracts, meetings of the "whole collective" — which includes both labor and management — are supposed to be held every three months
for "mass supervision" of their fulfillment. Workers' criticisms at these meetings and in letters to the
press may be sharp, and names may be named. At a
1951 meeting of the All-Union Central Council of
Trade Unions, reported in the labor newspaper
Trud, it was resolved that: "Ignoring signals of the
workers and criticism in the press, the minister of
the tractor industry, Comrade Khlamov, and the
president of the central council of the union of
workers in that industry, Comrade Blinov, did not
improve very serious shortcomings in the field of
protection of labor."

The Soviet worker may actively participate in the
total life of the factory. He shares directly in both
its responsibilities and its benefits. Although it is

not true to say that the factory belongs to him, he belongs to the factory, and his sense of belonging gives him status. It is this status which explains both the hardships to which he is subjected and the protection which he is accorded.

4

The Soviet Family

"REACTIONARIES are against freedom of divorce and call for a 'careful handling' of it, crying that it signifies 'the disintegration of the family.' But democrats know that the reactionaries are being hypocritical . . . that in fact freedom of divorce signifies not the 'disintegration' of family ties but on the contrary the strengthening of them on the only possible firm democratic foundation in a civilized society."

These words of Lenin reflect the Soviet view of the family in the first years after the Bolshevik Revolution of 1917. Russian leaders then believed that by removing both the legal and economic bonds of family life they would make possible the development of "true monogamy" and "true family unity"; in a socialist society the family would be transformed into a free association bound only by the free will of the members.

This conception underlay the Soviet Family Code of 1926, in which both marriage and divorce were made a matter of private agreement. Marriage was treated in law as a *de facto* relationship; registration of marriage, although encouraged, was not essential. Similarly, divorce could be accomplished merely by factual separation — although, again, the husband and wife were encouraged to notify the Bureau of Vital Statistics, at least by post card.

The liberalization of marriage and divorce was part of a larger program leading to the ultimate "withering away of the family" — that is, of the family as a legal and economic institution. Inheritance was at first declared to be abolished, and was later reintroduced with very severe restrictions. Extramarital children were given full equality with those born in wedlock. Abortions were legalized and could be obtained free of charge at state hospitals. Women were relieved of practically all legal and economic disabilities, in an effort to emancipate them from dependence upon men and from "the slavery of the kitchen."

It was thought that eventually children would be brought up by the state. "Our State institutions of guardianship," wrote the principal draftsman of early Soviet family legislation, "must show parents that the social care of children gives far better results than the private, individual, inexpert and irrational care of individual parents who are 'loving' but, in the matter of bringing up children, ignorant."

In the mid-1930's the theory that the "socialist family" would not be bound by legal and economic ties was officially denounced as a "left deviation." This rightabout-face in theory, with its wide practical implications, was associated with many other fundamental changes which took place at about the same time, including the return to Russian patriotism and to national traditions, the re-emphasis of rights of personal property, and the general restoration of law as a means of social control.

The return to family ties was also a direct response to practical family problems created in part by the earlier attitudes and policies. Juvenile delinquency had greatly increased, at least in the large cities, and in 1935 laws were passed imposing certain liabilities on parents for the crimes and civil wrongs of their children. Parental authority, deliberately undermined by the Bolsheviks in their earlier drive to turn the children away from pre-revolutionary beliefs and values, was now stressed as a necessary feature of a "socialist upbringing."

The abortion rate in some cities had come to exceed the birth rate, and in 1936 abortions were prohibited except in cases when continuation of the pregnancy seriously endangered the life or health of the mother, or when the parents had a dangerous disease which could be transferred by heredity.

The 1936 law on abortions also provided benefits for mothers of large families and instituted a system of progressively increasing fees for successive registered divorces. (There were 38.3 divorces per 100 marriages in Moscow in the first half of 1935, according to Soviet reports.) The juxtaposition of abortions, motherhood benefits, and divorce, indicate that the entire subject of Soviet family life was under review, and that population policy and family instability were considered as different aspects of the same problem.

The charging of fees for registered divorces could not solve the problem of *de facto* divorces, however, and although in the late 'thirties and early 'forties the courts became stricter in their requirements for proof of *de facto* marriages and divorces, it still remained true that many couples married for convenience — to obtain better living quarters in a crowded city, for example — and divorced at their leisure.

Finally, in 1944, a new family law established a judicial process of divorce, for the first time since the 1917 Revolution. Registration of marriage was made compulsory, with provision of a "solemn procedure" and "suitable premises properly furnished." The responsibility of fathers for support of children born out of wedlock was eliminated. In addition, the new law vastly increased the system of bonuses and medals for mothers of large families and set up a system of monthly state allowances for unmarried mothers.

Connected with the changes in family law was
the introduction in 1943 of separate education for
boys and girls through the tenth grade, with emphasis on teaching girls needlework, domestic
science, and the care of children. Also, in 1943 inheritance taxes were reduced to a maximum of 10
per cent, and in 1945 the system of succession was
greatly liberalized to permit family savings to be
kept intact and to extend the freedom of testamen-
tary disposition.

Not only did the 1944 legislation introduce judicial divorce procedure for the first time since the
Revolution, but it introduced *secular* judicial divorce procedure for the first time in Russian history — since prior to 1917 marriage and divorce
were a matter of ecclesiastical law exclusively.

The new Soviet divorce procedure, though secular, borrows certain features from the Russian religious tradition. Russian Orthodox ecclesiastical
law regards marriage as a sacrament, and divorce,
therefore, as a breach of the divine order of things,
justified only in exceptional circumstances. Soviet
law has not adopted the Russian Orthodox list of

grounds for divorce, but it treats divorce as a kind of fall from grace, a breach of the socialist ideal, to be granted only when the marriage has completely failed. Further, Soviet divorce law, like that of the Orthodox Church, places stress on a reconciliation procedure.

Whether or not a Soviet divorce is contested, both spouses must appear at a preliminary reconciliation hearing in the People's Court. Only if the defendant is insane, or missing, or serving a criminal sentence, is this requirement waived. The court is obliged to question the parties to ascertain the reasons for seeking a divorce, and to attempt to effect a reconciliation.

In discussing the measures which the People's Court should take to reconcile the parties, a Soviet commentator has stated: "It is impossible to expect any ready-made recipes. Here experience, tact, and the authority of the court are necessary. Far from always do the spouses come into court with a firm decision to separate. Often the suit is the result of a recent quarrel, the product of impetuousness and not a thought-out decision. Some the court may reconcile by means of a quiet explanation of the incorrectness of their behavior; it may convince others of the necessity of explaining to each other in court and forgiving each other; and to others it may give time for reconsideration."

"Why shouldn't I have the right to have other men?" asked a defendant in a case recently reported by a French observer. "Marriage is a serious thing, comrade," replied the judge, "not a casual pastime."

There are only scattered indications of the results of these reconciliation efforts, and no reports of the actual divorce rate in Russia today. In 1947 one author admonished the Ukrainian courts for their "light-hearted attitude" toward reconciliation, and complained that in 309 divorce cases in the Kiev region in the first quarter of 1947, only seven were settled by reconciliation. Another author writing in 1949 stated that in two Ukrainian regions reconciliation was effected in 54 per cent and 56 per cent of the cases.

That the reconciliation procedure is taken seriously is indicated by the fact that the Supreme

Court of the U.S.S.R. has, on several occasions, set aside divorce decrees on the ground that the preliminary hearing was incomplete.

If no reconciliation is effected, either spouse (or both) may file a petition for divorce in the next higher court.

The Family Code states no grounds for divorce, leaving it to the discretion of the court. From the reports of the cases and from Soviet legal treatises and articles, it is possible to detect the gradual emerging of a judge-made tradition of divorce law, similar to the growth of certain phases of English or American common law.

A general principle was laid down by the Soviet Supreme Court in a 1949 directive to lower courts that "temporary family discords and conflicts caused by accidental and transitory circumstances or the unwillingness of one or both spouses to continue the marriage, when not based on serious considerations, cannot be deemed sufficient grounds for divorce." Similarly, Soviet writers have stated that "divorce should be granted only in those cases where it is actually impossible to re-establish the broken family, where the breach between the spouses is so deep that it is impossible . . . to prolong their married life."

In application to various types of cases, such principles develop into more specific rules and doctrines. Mere incompatibility is not enough where there are minor children, even though the divorce is uncontested. The plaintiff may not rely on his own infidelity as a ground for a contested divorce. "The relationships which were created in the family, for which the plaintiff was himself responsible," the Supreme Court declared in reversing the decision of a lower court, "cannot serve as the basis for a divorce. The decision of the [lower] court in this case sanctions in substance the clearly amoral relationship of V. to his family duties, and it cannot be accepted as correct." Thus a moral element is introduced into Soviet divorce law.

On the other hand, the adultery or other guilt of the plaintiff will not rule out the divorce if "reestablishment of marital relations is impossible of achievement." In cases where the marriage had "factually terminated," as where the defendant had

deserted, or where the plaintiff had actually established another family, the courts have granted divorces. "There is no use in setting aside the decision," the Supreme Court declared pragmatically
in one such case.

Divorce is expensive in the Soviet Union. The
plaintiff must pay a fee of 100 rubles for filing the
divorce petition, as well as the cost of a notice in
the newspaper. Upon the granting of a divorce,
a fee of 500 to 2000 rubles is charged — theoretically, as a fine imposed on the "guilty" party;
actually it is usually levied against the plaintiff.
Five hundred rubles, despite the increase in wage
and price levels since the 1944 statute, is still more
than many Soviet workers, and most Soviet peasants, earn in a month.

Concepts of civil obligation of contract and
tort play a very minor role, if any, in Soviet divorce law. Anglo-American doctrines preventing
the granting of a divorce in cases where the peti-
tioner has "connived" with, or "condoned" the mis-
conduct of the respondent, or where there has been
"collusion" or "recrimination," are entirely alien

to Soviet law, while the common American practice of granting uncontested divorces automatically is equally foreign.

The Soviet concept of divorce is based upon the idea that the courts in granting or denying divorce should play a positive role in promoting family unity and responsibility. "Legal decisions in divorce cases are of great social-educational importance," stated *Pravda* in October 1949. The opinion of a prominent Western critic, writing in 1946, that "the new Soviet divorce procedure resembles the medieval pillory" is a gross distortion, but it contains a kernel of truth.

Soviet divorce procedure must be seen in the light of Soviet family legislation as a whole. Between 1944 and 1951, 33,000 Soviet women had received the Order of Mother Heroine of the Soviet Union and the substantial bonuses and allowances that go with it, for having given birth to and reared ten or more children. Over three million others, having five children or more, have received the Motherhood Medal or the Order of the Glory of Motherhood. The 1949 state budget provided 3,400,000,000 rubles for maternity benefits; the 1950 budget provided 4,000,000,000 rubles.

At the same time, there has been no substantial change in the policy toward working women, no positive effort to encourage them to leave the factory or the professions. There are over 190,000 Soviet women doctors and dentists and over 380,-000 women engineers and technicians. In the last war, 120,000 Soviet women won combat decorations. There are probably more women judges than men in the lower courts, and in the Supreme Court of the U.S.S.R., with approximately sixty members, there are some fourteen women. In addition, Soviet women dig ditches, lay bricks, work in the fields, and perform many other heavy manual labors.

The program of maternity benefits has not caused any apparent letup in the program of crèches, nurseries, and other aids to working mothers. Their legal independence has not been curtailed; their separate property rights have even been enhanced by the ruling that maternity bonuses belong to the mother individually.

But education and propaganda, implemented with material incentives, have definitely shifted their emphasis toward parental responsibility, filial devotion, marital fidelity, the family and the home. "A woman who has not yet known the joy of motherhood has not yet realized all the greatness of her calling," declared *Pravda* in welcoming the 1944 family legislation.

Today, according to a leading Soviet writer on the family, ". . . the people of the U.S.S.R. are convinced that not only in a socialist, but even in a perfect communist society, nobody will be able to replace the parents — the loving father and mother." In spite of Lenin, Soviet leaders now call for a "careful handling" not only of divorce but of family instability in general; they believe their own experience to have taught that the absence of legal and economic safeguards signifies "the disintegration of the family."

5

Soviet Education

MANY Soviet displaced persons in Western Europe and America count the Soviet system of education as the best feature of the Soviet social order. Certainly tremendous emphasis is placed upon education both by the rulers and the ruled. The regime has an immediate interest in the training of specialists to carry out its program of rapid economic, political and military expansion, as well as a long-range interest in molding the "new Soviet man." The people have different but parallel interests: to attain the economic and social privileges of the new Soviet intelligentsia, and to satisfy their own genuine thirst for knowledge.

Soviet leaders have given no indication that they share the fear attributed to an early nineteenth-century tsarist minister of education, that "to teach the mass of people, or even the majority of them, how to read will bring more harm than good." Despite rapid strides toward popular education in the latter nineteenth and early twentieth century, 67 per cent of the people of Russia were illiterate in 1914. In 1939 less than 20 per cent were illiterate, and of those more than half were over fifty years of age. With the end of World War II, strong measures were undertaken to combat increases in illiteracy caused by wartime disruptions of schooling.

The reduction of illiteracy has been accomplished largely by the introduction of universal compulsory education through the seventh grade. The school population of Russia in 1914 was under eight million; in 1939, with a total population increase of about 20 per cent, the school population was over thirty-two million.

Equally impressive is the increase in facilities for higher education. In 1914 there were in Russia about 90 institutions of higher education, with about 110,000 students. In 1952 there were some 900 institutions of higher education, with about 974,000 full-time students.

A small percentage of Soviet children between the ages of three and seven go to kindergarten, for which a small tuition fee must be paid. Compulsory schooling starts at the age of seven, and goes through seven grades. Those who intend to go on enter so-called ten-year schools, instead of the seven-year schools. The avowed aim of Soviet educators, from the beginning, has been to make the ten-year education compulsory. Nevertheless, in 1940 tuition fees — 200 rubles a year in Moscow, Leningrad, and the capitals of the republics, 150 rubles elsewhere — were introduced for the eighth, ninth, and tenth grades, with exemptions for certain groups, such as children of disabled veterans. Even before this, however, less than 20 per cent went on from seventh grade to "junior high."

Some — probably less than 8 per cent — of the graduates of the seven-year school go to special four-year professional and technical high schools (technicums), to be trained as junior specialists in some branch of science, industry, the arts, medicine, education, and the like. There the tuition fees are the same as for the eighth, ninth, and tenth grades.

Something like 20 per cent of the graduates of the seven-year school are conscripted into the State Labor Reserves for four years, where they receive free on-the-job schooling. Thus over half the Soviet youth discontinue their formal education at the end of the seventh grade, at about the age of fourteen.

Upon graduation from ten-year secondary schools and from professional and technical high schools (and usually after two years of military training), roughly one out of five enters higher educational institutions for specialized training. Admission is on the basis of nation-wide competitive examinations. Tuition fees are from 300 to 500 rubles a year — again, with exemptions for certain groups including Heroes of the Soviet Union and Heroes of Socialist Labor, as well as "A" students. Stipends are paid to "good" students, who comprise about 80 per cent of the total number.

As in Europe generally, there is no liberal arts college. A higher educational institution falls into one of the following categories: industry and construction, transport and communications, agriculture, public health, teacher training, social sciences, the arts. The emphasis is on the training of specialists — though that training is by no means narrow. Only about 10 per cent of the Soviet colleges are devoted to either the arts or the social sciences.

Moscow University, with over 14,000 students, including those taking correspondence courses, has eleven different divisions and trains students in fifty different specialties. Leningrad University is slightly larger. Other large universities are at Tiflis, Kiev, Riga (formerly Latvian), and Lvov (formerly Polish). All told there are twenty-three city universities.

The organization of Soviet schools and colleges is highly centralized. The general pattern is set by the Council of Ministers of the U.S.S.R., which issues decrees (sometimes coauthored by the Central Committee of the Communist Party) allocating funds and determining basic educational policies. Institutions of higher education are directly under the All-Union Ministry of Higher Education. Most of the other schools are under the Ministry of Education of the republic in which they are situated. Teachers are appointed and given their salaries — which are quite low in the Soviet scale — by the ministry through its local branches.

The ministries of education implement decisions of the Council of Ministers through detailed instructions which cover every aspect of the curriculum. The ideal traditionally attributed in France to the Minister of Education — to be able to look at his watch and tell what page every French school-boy is reading — is apparently shared in the Soviet Union.

For example, the Ministry of Education of the R.S.F.S.R. has set forth a syllabus for botany for the fifth grade, which starts as follows:

Introduction (1 hour). Botany — science of the structure and life of plants. Botany in the service of Socialist construction.

(1) *General acquaintance with the flowering plant* (4 hours). Organs of the flowering plant. Cellular structure of plants. Conception of the plant cell. *Laboratory work:* (a) study of the external structure of a flowering plant; (b) acquaintance with the cellular structure of plants (work with magnifying glass). *Demonstration:*

the plant cell under the microscope (onion skin). *Excursion* for a general acquaintance with flowering plants.

(2) *The Seed, its germination and the preparation of seeds for sowing* (10 hours). The structure of the seeds of dicotyledons and monocotyledons. Composition of seeds. Alteration of the seed and its parts during germination. Conditions necessary for germination. Respiration of germinating seeds. The determination of viability and purity of the sowing material. . . .

The syllabus then goes on in elaborate detail to state the subjects to be treated, together with the laboratory work, demonstrations, experiments and excursions to be undertaken, with regard to the root, the leaf, the stem, reproduction, and growth and development of plants. Altogether 65 hours are allotted; 130 would not seem too many to cover adequately the materials set forth.

In the words of the British scientist Eric Ashby, a close observer of Soviet education, "There is only one way to get through such a formidable syllabus, that is the didactic way, with *ex cathedra* statement; learning by heart; and in science the minimum of experiment and discussion. This is the way which is in fact adopted in spite of the admirable exhortations in each syllabus."

Each course has its syllabus, from first grade up through postgraduate studies. There is no choice of subjects. From the fourth grade on there are national examinations, written and oral, held at particular times throughout the country. At the end of the ten-year school, students are examined in the following subjects: Russian language, literature, mathematics (algebra, geometry, trigonometry), physics, chemistry, history (history of the U.S.S.R., modern history), and a foreign language. In non-Russian-speaking areas an examination is also given in the students' native language. Besides the subjects in which there are examinations before graduation, the ten-year school curriculum includes natural history, geography, Constitution of the U.S.S.R., astronomy, military and physical training, design, drawing, and singing.

Since 1940, either English, German or French is required from the fifth grade on. Which language is taught in any school depends on the teacher; in one school it may be English only, in another

German. In addition, there is at least one Soviet
school where the language of instruction is English, and the students while in school are supposed
to converse with each other only in English. Latin,
which was reintroduced in the law schools and
some other higher educational institutions in the
'thirties, was in 1952 restored in the secondary
schools as well.

With education as with almost everything else
of importance in Soviet society, it has not always
been so. Soviet education in the 'twenties and early
'thirties was dominated by radical ideas similar to
those which have caused a stir in the United States.
Emphasis was on "spontaneous education," "learning from life"; the classroom was conceived as a
kind of laboratory, in which the teacher organized
the work around projects, many of which were
left to the pupils' own initiative. Instruction was
played down. Special subjects were not taught, but
instead were supposed to be learned incidentally,
by "doing." American educational experiments,
such as the Dalton Plan evolved by Helen Park-
hurst in Dalton, Massachusetts, and others under-

taken by the followers of John Dewey, had a great influence on this first phase of Soviet educational development. Characteristically, Soviet extremism made our reforms seem modest. The Soviets anticipated the gradual "withering away" of the school altogether. As one leading Soviet educator wrote in 1925:

In my opinion there will be no school in the future communist society. The child will go immediately into societal work . . . We will all be pedagogues. The child will go from societal work to industrial work, and from there to the library, where he will find the answers to all the questions which interest him. We are approaching closer and closer to this all the time.

By a series of sweeping decrees starting in 1932 and continuing through 1943 and 1944, Soviet progressive education has been almost entirely scrapped. A 1932 decree abolished the Dalton Plan and the project method, and introduced the three R's. In 1934 a decree on the teaching of history ordered "the observance of historical and chronological sequence in the exposition of historical events," and stated that facts, names, and dates

should receive due emphasis. In 1937 "polytech-
nism," that is, the organization of the curriculum
around labor, was under heavy fire. A decree of
the R.S.F.S.R. Ministry (then People's Commissariat) of Education abolished the teaching of labor
as an independent subject; the hours thus freed
were to be devoted to the Russian language, literature, mathematics, and the Constitution of the
U.S.S.R. Research in problems of polytechnics was
abandoned, and subjects of the conventional type
came to prevail in the curricula. By 1939 polytech-
nism was out, though the name crops up from time
to time.

In 1943 separate schools for boys and for girls
were introduced in eighty large cities, and later
elsewhere. "Coeducation," said the then People's
Commissar for Education, "makes no allowance for
differences in the physical development of boys and
girls, for variations required by the sexes in pre-
paring each for their future life work, for good
practical activity, for military training, and it does
not insure the required standard of discipline among
the pupils." However, coeducation was not com-

pletely abolished, and there has been a frank and vigorous debate in the Soviet press on the relative merits of the two systems. In 1950 a storm of letters on both sides was started by a professor who ridiculed some of the extremes to which separate education has gone; he quoted the headmistress of a girls' school as suggesting that under the names "physics in everyday life," "chemistry in everyday life," and so forth, girls should be taught how to repair an electric plate or an iron, how to make soap, and how to remove grease marks.

The proponents of separate education have stressed the practical desirability of military training for schoolboys and of special training for girls in homemaking and motherhood; more fundamentally, however, the argument has been that separate education promotes better discipline. A few weeks after the decree on separate education, the R.S.F.S.R. education authorities promulgated twenty "Rules for School Children," imposing obligations of conscientious study, good behavior in school and after school, neatness, respect for teachers, and so forth. Rule 9 states that pupils must rise when the teacher enters or leaves the room. Rule 12 requires that upon meeting a teacher on the streets students must give a polite bow, and the boys must remove their hats. A "pupil's card," on the back of which the rules are printed, must be carried at all times.

Also, discipline was encouraged by the reintroduction of the prerevolutionary marking system (with grades 1, 2, 3, 4, 5, representing "excellent," "good," "fair," "passing," and "failing"), the reintroduction of examinations, and the introduction of an examination for a Diploma in Maturity which must be passed before the student is graduated from grade ten. Articles and books on *The Authority of the Teacher* have appeared during and since the war. Punishments may now be administered, including admonition, ordering the delinquent to rise from his seat or to leave the room, and expulsion from school. "The absence of punishment demoralizes the will of the school child," *Pravda* stated in 1944. However, corporal punishment is forbidden — though it is apparently sometimes practiced.

The changes in educational policy in the past

fifteen to twenty years represent a new philosophy not only of education but of human nature itself. A 1936 decree of the Central Committee of the Party, which attacked psychological testing of school children, established the basic premises of the new educational policy by emphasizing the power of man, by training and self-training, to overcome both his heredity and his environment. Man can lift himself by his bootstraps. More than that, he is responsible for doing so — and for failing to do so. The new educational policy stresses the responsibility of the pupil or student. He is no longer an end in himself. His sense of duty must be actively directed and developed. As a Soviet educator and psychologist wrote in 1944, "The sense of duty is a special quality which underlies all other feelings in man, penetrating each of them, determining their strength."

The political implications of this philosophy are not concealed. The schools are required "to educate the youth in the spirit of unrestrained love for the Motherland and devotion to Soviet authority." The Young Communist League (Komsomol) with sixteen million members between the ages of fourteen and twenty-six, is supposed to "show the way" in combating "ideological neutrality." "The most important task of the Komsomol organization," states a handbook of 1947, "is to instil into all the youth Soviet patriotism, Soviet national pride, the aspiration to make our Soviet State even stronger."

The Komsomol was originally restricted to "class conscious and politically literate youth" from the proletariat and poorer peasantry. In 1936 the conditions of admission were changed from social origin to loyalty to the Soviet regime. Further, Komsomol leaders were then called on to organize athletic competitions, musical events, plays, dances, evening literary discussions, and other cultural activities, and not to concentrate only on political work. Following these changes, membership jumped from four million in 1936 to nine million in 1939. In 1945 membership was reported to be fifteen million — roughly half the eligible age group. However, in 1949 membership dropped to a little over nine million, and the Soviet press has complained of the indifference of the youth to Komsomol membership. In October

1952 the membership was reported to be sixteen million.

The Komsomol is a stepping stone to the Party — though the majority of its members do not go on to join the Party. The Young Pioneers, a still less selective group with some nineteen million members between the ages of nine and fifteen, is a stepping-stone to the Komsomol. Children under nine are enrolled in the "Little Octobrists." All these youth organizations are a totalitarian version of our Boy Scout clubs. The Komsomol Handbook of 1947 requires its members to "obey Soviet laws" and to "give active support to the organs of authority." The appeal is to "friendship," "politeness," and also to "heroism" and "a socialist attitude toward work, founded on an iron conscious discipline." Premilitary training is considered an important part of Komsomol activities.

The patriotic, military, and moral emphasis of Komsomol and school activity is implemented by indoctrination in Marxist theory, as redefined by Lenin and Stalin. Political propaganda permeates the curriculum. School children are taught the superi-

ority of the "Soviet" biology of Michurin and Ly-
senko over "bourgeois" biology. In studying Shake-
speare, students are taught Marx's views of the
development of English capitalism; *Hamlet* is seen
in part as an exposure of a decadent court aristocracy. "Marxism-Leninism" is a required course
in all Soviet institutions of higher education. Doctors' dissertations in all fields must be ideologically
correct, and there is even some indication that de-
grees may be revoked years later if "mistakes" in
them are discovered.

It is not clear to what extent political-ideological
considerations affect the selection of students for
institutions of higher education. Prior to 1935 and
1936, social origin was a decisive factor: the son of
"bourgeois" parents could easily become a doctor,
but only with difficulty could he become an engineer. Also great stress was laid on ideological re-
liability in school advancement. This changed in the
mid-1930's after a famous speech by Stalin in which
he said, "Children should not suffer for the sins of
their fathers." Today in many fields, perhaps in
most, education is open to talent. Of course "pull"

remains a very important factor: the son of a high Party official gets many privileges in education as elsewhere. Also any indication of dissent from Party doctrine can have serious consequences extending even to imprisonment. But for the student without high Party connections, the main criterion in admission to engineering schools or law schools or agronomist schools or teachers colleges, is ability, as manifested in examinations — including, of course, the examination in Marxism-Leninism.

Also the increased authority of the teacher has contributed to the toning down of political-ideological considerations in the treatment of students. In an earlier time it was common for teachers to live in fear that their students might report them to the Party for alleged non-Marxist statements. That fear still exists, but it has greatly diminished. For example, one former Soviet doctor now in this country states:

"In 1935 a medical student might tell an assistant professor who was explaining reactions of immunity, 'That is not right; it contradicts the theory of dialectical materialism, and therefore it is not true.' In

1940 such a thing would not have been possible, and the teacher would have been able to expel the student for being disrespectful. He might expel him from the classroom and it might even result in his expulsion from the university."

Still, the teacher must be careful to teach the Party line. How successful such indoctrination is may be seriously questioned. A 1952 Soviet publication states:

There are institutes where the lectures on Marxism-Leninism are delivered in a perfunctory manner, without relation to current events. Individual teachers do not see the spirit behind the letter, and present the subject matter in a mechanical fashion

With the doctrine so stereotyped and dogmatized, it is difficult to see how it could be otherwise. Professor Boris Konstantinovsky, a Soviet D.P. who taught law in Odessa from 1926 to 1944, says that he did not believe the propaganda which he was compelled to teach, the students knew he did not believe it — and knew that he knew that they knew!

6

Soviet Medical Care

LIKE Soviet education, Soviet medical care has undergone phenomenal expansion since the Revolution. In 1913 there were 20,000 doctors in Tsarist Russia; in Soviet Russia there were 63,000 doctors in 1928, 112,000 in 1938, 130,000 in 1941, 180,000 in 1948, and about 215,000 in 1951. The number of medical centers increased from 5600 in 1913 to 27,000 in 1941; the number of hospital beds increased from 142,000 in 1913 to 661,000 in 1941 and 694,000 in 1946. These figures do not include maternity hospital beds, of which there were 140,-000 in 1946.

This expansion has favored the cities more than the villages. For example, of the 694,000 hospital beds in 1946, only 185,000 were in the villages — although the total rural population is roughly twice the urban population. The serious shortage of doctors in the villages is somewhat compensated by the existence of the *feldsher*, a medical assistant with a three-year secondary education; the village *feldsher* — roughly comparable to a U.S. Public Health Nurse — is often the only doctor the village has.

The U.S.S.R. Ministry of Health seeks to meet the problem of maldistribution of medical care by assigning doctors to villages for three years, after graduation from medical school. The rural doctor's somewhat higher salary provides a material incentive. However, there is little to buy in the villages, and the cultural and living standards are low. As a result a very large percentage of doctors find excuses — legitimate and otherwise — for avoiding village service. The commonest legitimate excuse is marriage; under Soviet law a married woman cannot be compelled to leave her husband's place of residence — and this applies equally to women doctors, who comprise over half (some estimates go up to 70 per cent) of the total Soviet medical profession.

Apart from assignment upon graduation, there is no direct compulsion of doctors to engage in a particular type of practice or to work in particular places. Upon completion of three years of assigned practice, and in some cases earlier, the doctor may choose a field of specialization, and the law requires that he be sent for training in that field. Alternatively, he is encouraged to take a general medical refresher course. Thereafter he is entitled to take refresher courses at periodic intervals, though this is often frustrated by the lack of a replacement for him. According to a former Soviet doctor who chose not to return to Russia, it is not difficult for physicians in the U.S.S.R. who have ability and "who are not interested in money" to receive a higher qualification — that is, as specialists, clinic residents, research workers, and professors. Many go into the armed forces. Advancement to important positions outside of medical administration usually depends on merit as demonstrated in competitive examinations. Party membership has apparently not been a significant factor since about 1936, except in administrative positions. About 20 per cent of Soviet doctors are Party members, and those are chiefly in administration.

The doctor's freedom is limited, however, by the planned character of Soviet medical care; the U.S.S.R. Ministry of Health — which is in charge of hospitals and medical centers, sanitation, medical education and research, the medical instrument industry, and all aspects of public health — determines not only the quota of students admitted to medical schools and training courses each year, but also the numbers and types of jobs available to doctors. All Soviet physicians are employed by state agencies under the jurisdiction of the Ministry of Health and its local branches. More than half are employed in medical centers — urban polyclinics (for out patients), ambulatoria (for nonbedridden patients), medical stations for first aid and the like, and specialized treatment centers for tuberculosis, cancer, mental diseases, skin and venereal diseases, and so forth.

Doctors are paid on the basis of salary scales set by the Council of Ministers. Under a 1942 decree, head physicians of hospitals and medical centers receive 750 to 1400 rubles per month, depending on the number of beds or the number of calls per year; physicians in cities receive 500 to 725 rubles per month; physicians in rural areas receive 550 to 850 per month; *feldshers* receive 325 to 500 rubles per month, depending in part on the length of their education; dentists with higher education receive the same salaries as doctors, while graduates of dental institutes receive less and graduates of secondary dental schools still less. The 1942 decree sets the wages of junior medical workers and service personnel, such as sanitation workers, bathhouse attendants, and morgue attendants, at 200 to 260 rubles per month. Managers of city pharmacies with higher pharmaceutical education are paid from 600 to 1000 rubles per month, depending on the number of prescriptions filled per year.

These official salary scales for doctors compare unfavorably with those for engineers, skilled technicians, skilled industrial workers, and many other groups; they compare favorably with those of teachers, minor government officials, and ordinary workers and peasants. Like many other Soviet professionals, the doctor is apt to take more than one job in order to make a living. In addition, he is apt to take gifts from his patients. One Soviet doctor is reported by a former Soviet citizen to have said: "I like to deal with collective farmers because they always bring something with them." Such a gift is illegal if it is a bribe for special consideration. Careful Soviet doctors report offers of bribes, if only out of fear that the patient may be a police informer.

On the other hand, a Soviet specialist may legally carry on a private practice on the side. Although medical care is free (except that a small charge is now made for medicines), many patients are willing to pay for treatment by particular specialists. Income from private practice is subject to high taxes.

The difficulty in generalizing about such matters as bribery of doctors is illustrated in the following account given by a former Soviet physician now in this country, who had practiced both in Siberia and in Kiev. "In Siberia," he states, "none of the doctors who called at patients' homes ever took money that the patients gave as a token of gratitude for the visit. Not only did they not accept money, they did not even take food. In Kiev I saw the doctors willingly accepting money offered them, and I do not doubt that there were many cases when they gave certificates of illness [excusing the patient from work and entitling him to social insurance] because the patient had offered money . . . They thought, If I don't give the certificate this fellow will suffer, but by giving this document I am taking a risk. Therefore, I take money for the risk. In Siberia I never saw anything like that. I explained this to myself later by the fact that the population of Siberia is morally much cleaner than that of the Ukrainian big cities."

The pressure from patients for doctors to issue certificates of illness — and from management to refuse to issue them — is probably the worst feature of Soviet medical practice. Medical centers are generally associated with individual industries, enterprises, or other organizations. Thus a railroad employee who is ill would normally go to a railroad medical center; a steel worker would go to the medical center attached to the steel plant or its superior organization. With the 1940 laws imposing criminal penalties for lateness and absenteeism "without adequate reason," the medical excuse signed by the doctor has become an object of intense political, economic, and legal interest. On the one hand, patients use every conceivable trick to deceive the doctor, or else to play on his sympathies; on the other hand management, and especially the Party organs supervising production, are apt to look on him as a saboteur if he grants too many excuses, however legitimate they may be.

As one former Soviet doctor put it: "A good 50 per cent of the cases at the railroad clinic where I worked were only fakers. A man wants to rest . . . or maybe he wants to stand in line and buy a coat or something. Or there were people who overslept and came late. Since one had to stand in line after shifts and work and cook, life was very hard. Thus sleep was a dead-man's sleep and it was hard to get up in the morning. Moreover, the majority of them had no watches. As soon as he sees he is late the worker will go directly to the doctor . . . They start dreaming up what is bothering them."

Another former Soviet doctor states: "There was a whole army of fakers, who knew the system and wanted, for example, to get a few days off to go fishing. They would come in and say they were sick. They put hot peppers or mustard seeds under their arms [where the thermometer is placed] and in that way they could deceive the doctor with a higher than normal temperature." Other reported methods of deception include injections of milk, taking large doses of drugs, self-inflicted wounds, and the like.

A third doctor reports: "In Georgia the small peasant household remained, with its little garden plot — even for workers who went into factories. And in the spring this plot has to be cultivated. And as soon as spring comes, and we all knew it, all the patients would try to fake illness. And even if a man had the grippe and you gave him five days off, a doctor who checked at his home would not find him there because he would have gone to the village."

To check leniency on the part of doctors, rigid requirements have been established by medical administrators. The patient must have a fever and the doctor must show the thermometer to the nurse. Further, quotas of certificates are established, and to grant any beyond the quota requires special permission.

The doctor is exhorted to concern himself not only with medicine but also with production. A 1947 article in the journal of the Ministry of Health, *Medical Worker*, states:

If the pre-revolutionary doctor was proud of the fact that for him "medicine" existed and nothing else . . . the Soviet doctor, on the other hand, is proud of the fact that he actively participates in the building of socialism.

Like certificates of illness, abortions — illegal except under strictly defined circumstances — also put the Soviet doctor in the dilemma of breaking the law (and in this case risking up to six years in a labor camp) or refusing to alleviate economic hardship. Former Soviet doctors report many instances of patients begging for abortions on the ground of the difficulty of feeding, clothing, and housing another child.

Official pressure upon the doctor is by no means directed only *against* the patient; it may also be invoked *for* the patient. The Ministry of Health has a central Bureau of Complaints, to which any person may protest against rudeness or negligence on the part of a doctor. Complaints are also made to local health departments and to the Union of Medical Workers, as well as to the chief law-enforcement agency, the Procuracy. Sometimes these complaints are written up in provincial and local newspapers.

For example, the journal *Medical Worker* of January 13, 1952, under the caption "Only Heartless?" published a letter telling of a woman who complained of pains in the region of the liver and was hospitalized. After a month and a half in which she received practically no attention, her protests brought down the wrath of the physician, one Professor Voronov, who charged her with malingering. She was discharged and went to another clinic where she received the medical care she needed. Her son, the writer of the letter, concludes: "Of course, one cannot require that in each case the doctor make a faultless diagnosis. But it is completely intolerable that when a doctor cannot determine the illness he should insult the patient. This is precisely the way Dr. Cherkessova [the subject of another such complaint] and Professor Voronov acted with their patients. This is called heartless. Is that all?"

Another letter, in the trade-union newspaper *Trud*, relates: "In the Sanatorium of the Trade Union No. 1 at Tskhaltubo the patients see the doctor [only] when they arrive and when they leave . . . Comrades Panus, Goncharov, Kitani and others complain about the rudeness of Comrade Kuznetsov, the chief doctor of the Odessa sanatorium. . . ."

In a 1951 article *Trud* stated: "Every example of a careless attitude toward the patient, every instance of insolence and irresponsibility, must become the subject of public investigation and action." Actually, only the more serious complaints are investigated, usually by a commission of the Ministry of Health. If it is shown that the doctor is at fault he may be reprimanded or, in more important cases, removed from his position. The Union, which includes not only doctors but all persons working for the Ministry of Health, may impose informal semi-criminal penalties. If the patient suffers serious harm as a result of the doctor's negligence, the public prosecutor is apt to institute criminal proceedings; also the patient may bring a civil action for malpractice.

As hard as the pressures of public criticism and official supervision may be on the doctor, more serious from the patient's point of view is the scarcity of medical equipment, drugs, and other facilities, and the poor quality of medical instruments. These factors are difficult to measure, but their existence is demonstrated both by reports of Soviet *émigrés* and by letters and statements in official Soviet literature. The press carries stories under such headings as: "They Don't Care About the Clinic," "Disorder and Waste," "Once More About the [Bad] Quality of Hypodermic Needles." In addition, the quality of medical care is by no means always high; Soviet doctors are turned out too fast and in too large numbers to maintain the highest standards. The situation is aggravated by the fact that the best doctors and best medical facilities are reserved for high Party officials and their relatives.

In spite of all the difficulties they face, Soviet doctors seem to have both self-respect and the respect of the people. Soviet displaced persons indicate that medical care ranks second only to education as a "positive" feature of the Soviet system. A Soviet *émigré* doctor, who received his medical training after the Revolution and practiced in Russia until near the end of the war, states: "We were convinced that the best part of the Soviet system was the medical set-up and that there was no region of activity of the country which was so well structured as medical care, insofar as the Soviet people are concerned. I have had a chance to compare medical work in the Soviet Union with similar work in Poland and Germany, and also have a certain knowledge of the French system and have had the opportunity of observing the system in the United States, and it appears to me that health protection in the Soviet Union was as well structured as in Germany and that the German and the Soviet systems are better than the ones in the other countries I mentioned."

Asked to explain the alleged superiority of the Soviet system of medical care, the doctor attributed it largely to the "missionary spirit" of Soviet physicians, who are by and large not interested in money — of which they receive relatively little. "Only people with high idealism would accept work for such minimal salaries," he states. Asked what kind of ethics were taught in the medical schools, he replied:

"Ethics were taught continually. Russian medicine has one thesis which has been followed from the beginning. This thesis is made up of the following points: 1) There is no disease in the individual, there is a sick person. 2) The moral and spiritual condition of the patient has a great deal of influence upon sickness. 3) The doctor is the better the more he loves his patient, for without love there is no confidence in a doctor and this is the basic tenet of Russian medicine. We were taught always to remember that we would deal with people. This kind of teaching created an effective missionary spirit.

"For example, the low pay that we received caused wonder among engineers and other technicians. They asked us why we had entered medical school. In one of the big Siberian industrial towns an engineer asked me, 'Why do they pay the doctors so little?' This question was asked not only in astonishment but also with fun and irony. I understood this irony and answered in this way: 'In our country the people receive salaries depending on the kind of materials with which they work . . .' They were rather dismayed by this kind of answer and they thought it over. Then I added, 'I do not work for money, but for the gratitude which I will get when you are sick, not from you but from your wife.' I noticed afterwards that the attitude of these engineers changed radically towards the doctors. They understood the quality of this missionary spirit."

A former inmate of a Soviet labor camp, writing in France in 1950, says that she was told by a camp doctor: "The camp is made to tighten the screws on the prisoners, and we doctors are here to loosen them a bit."

7

The Soviet Press

IF a man bites a dog, that's news — but not in the Soviet Union. If a dog bites a man, that might well be the occasion for an article in a Soviet newspaper on the increase in number of household pets, the importance of taking a socialist attitude toward their care, and the necessity for expansion of facilities for the detection and prevention of rabies.

The Soviet press is conceived primarily as a means of organizing and educating the people. No distinction is drawn between straight reporting and editorializing. Every article is supposed to interest the reader in the social, economic, political, and cultural development of the country. As Alex Inkeles has said, it is not events that are considered newsworthy, but social processes; events are regarded as being news only insofar as they can meaningfully be related to social processes.

The average Soviet newspaper — there are some 7000 of them, with a circulation of over 30 million — would seem extraordinarily dull to the average American reader. Not only are there no reports of crimes and divorces, and rarely any account of the personal lives of individuals named, but more fundamentally there is no attempt to give a picture of what happened yesterday. It does not bother a Soviet editor if he is weeks late in publishing the report of some event. Contrast some headlines from a typical issue of the *New York Times:* "Eisenhower To Back McCarthy If Named But Assails Tactics," "California Quake Ruins Part of City; 2 to 5 Feared Dead," "Mayor Condemns Queens Sewer Job," "Soviet Offers U.S. 10-Story Site For Its New Embassy in Moscow" — with some from a typical issue of *Pravda:* "The Growth of the Economy and Culture of the Soviet Republic" (an account of progress made during 1951), "For Shortening the Production Cycle" (a report of Stakhanovite initiative in a particular machine-construction plant), "Rest Homes in Kirgizia" (a brief mention of several sanatoria for workers), "Millionnaire Collective Farms" (another progress report), "The Propagation of Scientific Information" (a report on a recently opened planetarium in Kiev), "On the Hundredth Anniversary of Gogol" (plans for celebration). Much of the foreign news, which generally takes up about 40 per cent of *Pravda's* four pages of space, is usually more in the style of our straight news reporting. The foreign news dispatches are apt to be very short and terse.

Pravda is one of twenty-five central, or all-union, newspapers, which together account for about one fourth of total newspaper circulation. It is published as the organ of the Central Committee of the Communist Party, and in 1949 had a circulation of about two-and-one-half million. *Izvestiya*, with a much smaller circulation (800,000 in 1947) is the organ of the Supreme Soviet, that is, of the government as contrasted with the Party. Its coverage is not much different in kind from that of *Pravda*, except that it devotes somewhat more attention to governmental appointments and other matters of state administration. Other important central newspapers include

Red Star, the organ of the army, whose circulation in 1939 was 500,000; *Trud*, the organ of the Central Committee of the All-Union Council of Trade Unions, with a circulation in 1939 of 144,900; *Red Sport*, the organ of the physical culturists, with a circulation in 1939 of 50,300. All the papers carry general articles on foreign and domestic affairs, but each devotes special attention to the affairs of its particular sponsor. Except for Tass dispatches (mostly foreign) and the *Pravda* lead editorial (usually radioed to all papers), each has its own coverage.

Among the more general newspapers (like *Pravda* and *Izvestiya*) there are, on the regional level, such papers as the chief Ukrainian language newspaper, *Radianska Ukraina*, which had a circulation of 400,-000 in 1947, the *Leningrad Pravda*, the *Evening Moscow*, the *Turkmen Spark*. But by far the majority of Soviet papers are addressed to specialized audiences, such as peasants, soldiers, teachers, railway workers or, on the local level, workers of a particular plant. The weekly paper of the Gorkov auto plant had a circulation of 12,000 in 1947. Also the typewritten or handwritten wall newspaper of a factory, collective farm, office, military unit, or apartment house is treated as an important part of the Soviet press. Most Soviet newspapers are weeklies and have a small circulation, averaging about 2000.

The central newspapers control the regional and local papers. Papers published by regional trade-union councils and by particular industries and large factories follow the pattern set by *Trud* and are periodically criticized at conferences held by *Trud*. The republican and regional *Pravdas* have a similar relationship to the central *Pravda*. The daily paper of the Komsomols is parent to the 150 other youth papers throughout the country. *Red Star* directs the work of the numerous military district and unit newspapers.

The entire press is under the over-all control of the Department of Propaganda and Agitation of the Communist Party, which issues directives on all matters affecting Soviet public opinion. There is precensorship for security purposes, but otherwise reliance is placed on regular supervision and criticism after publication and on what might be called self-censorship. At the top, at least, no one has to tell the editor what to say in advance because the editor is himself part of the higher Party apparatus.

Despite the stereotype imposed by the system of control, and despite the press's lack of interest in news as such, a Russian who takes the trouble to read his paper or papers carefully (many read two, one general paper such as *Pravda* and a second "occupational" paper such as the railway paper, or the water transport paper) may learn a great deal about what is happening both at home and in the outside world.

He knows that he is reading what he is supposed to read, and estimates accordingly. By the mood and tone of the articles he can tell a good deal about what the top echelons are thinking. By the facts reported he can detect strong or weak spots in the economy and in the system. For example, a *Pravda* report of a session of the Moscow City Council, in which it is stated that the 1951 plan for introduction of gas for cooking and heating purposes was overfulfilled and that 85 per cent of the population of

Moscow now use gas, and which says nothing about further plans in this field, may tell him that if he is in the other 15 per cent he should not expect to have a gas stove in 1952.

An American student of Soviet affairs once remarked to former Ambassador Troyanovsky that he had observed a change in policy on a certain matter on the part of the Soviet government. Troyanovsky asked what made him think so. The American replied that he followed *Pravda*, and that in respect to the particular matter various points which in the past had been made in a certain order — one, two, three — were in a recent issue switched around in the order three, two, one. Troyanovsky replied: "Mr. H——, you have learned to read the Soviet press."

Furthermore, the Soviet reader gets his instructions, so to speak, from the press. Thus the *Pravda* lead article of February 5, 1952 (to take a random example), entitled "Raising the Culture of Publishing," begins with the usual "line" about how the Soviet Press, "the freest in the world," "carries to the masses the great ideas of Lenin-Stalin," but then gets down to business with praise and criticism of particular printing establishments. "Comrade Loti-val'tsev, Stakhanovite of the Leningrad printers 'Pechatnyi Dvor,' doubled the speed of the rotation machine and thus initiated the serving of three such machines by one printer. . . ." "The work of such publishers as" [and there follow the names of four publishing houses] "calls forth the serious critical comment of readers." And then there follow the instructions: "It is the duty of local party organizations daily and concretely to occupy themselves with the problem of publishing, propaganda, and the circulation of books and pamphlets, papers and magazines." Not only local party organizations but also workers and officials in the publishing business and allied fields know that "this means you."

A very large proportion of space in all Soviet newspapers is filled by reports of Stakhanovites who have speeded up production by one method or another. This is not just propaganda in the ordinary sense: it is vital information which affects the working lives of millions of Soviet citizens. If the happy, eager face of P. D. Sudnikov, who devised a new method of organizing the movement of freight cars in and around Minsk, appears in the two right-hand columns of *Pravda*, with an article telling how he did it, then engineers and administrators of railroads in other cities understand the implication: go thou and do likewise.

Since each newspaper is a "house organ," as Inkeles has called it, of the particular Party or government or economic agency that sponsors it, the readers know more or less to whom and for what the articles are directed, and are able to read between the lines for information as well as instructions. This is especially true of the occupational and local press.

In February 1952 the Ministry of River Transport held a conference of readers and "worker correspondents" — persons who pass on news to the press and support it in other ways — of the newspaper *River Transport*, published three times a week by the Ministry and its trade union. The editor spoke of the efforts made to overcome deficiencies pointed out by a *Pravda* article of June 26, 1951. The chief engineer of the Moscow Basin Construction Administration expressed the wish that the paper would help him more in his work of organizing the supply of materials and would devote more attention to reporting new developments. Comrade Iziumov of the Chief Administration of the Western Fleet said that only two or three articles had been devoted to a system of rewards for workers developed by Engineer Kovalev, that this was clearly not enough, and that the articles had been too academic. Others also called for more articles on Stakhanovite methods. Comrade Sabinin said that he read the paper with the eyes of a passenger, and that he would like more information on the opening of new lines, and also that more space should be devoted to stories, sketches, and poems. He suggested that a "literary page" appear from time to time. After these and other criticisms, the editor made a concluding speech in which he said in effect that he would do his best.

Reader interest is a matter of great concern to Soviet editors. Although the newspaper will not go out of business if circulation drops, the editors may. Also the financial side is not unimportant, especially since the postwar decree putting all publishing houses on a profit-and-loss basis. However, the principal reason for interest in circulation is the felt need to hammer home the Party's policies, from the most general matters of doctrine to concrete questions affecting, say, a change in particular work norms. In the light of these considerations, it is perhaps surprising that the press has restrained itself from providing more entertainment in its columns. Occasionally, a political cartoon will introduce a certain sardonic note, but otherwise the Soviet newspapers are almost completely humorless. Some diversion may be provided by the notices of radio programs and theater, concert and ballet performances, and by the detailed reports of state lotteries.

Also there is an occasional advertisement. The Chief Administration of State Insurance advertises fairly widely for life insurance: "Anyone may conclude a life insurance contract of various types for different periods of time and for any sum; to conclude a contract of insurance see the inspector or call an agent of State Insurance to your house." Another advertisement which appeared recently in the newspaper *River Transport* stated that the co-oper-

ative "30th October" accepts various turners' jobs in
metal, prepares pieces of furniture (locks, hinges),
buttons, darning and shoe needles, various wire
products — and a long list of other things. The co-
operative would conclude contracts for 1952; "cash
not necessary."

Probably the most interesting feature of Soviet
newspapers, not only to Soviet readers and officials
but also to foreign students of Soviet society, are the
letters to the editor. *Pravda* is reported to receive
200,000 letters a year, though it usually prints not
more than one every few days. Other newspapers
print more — *Evening Moscow* may on occasion
have four or five in a single issue. The letters are
mostly concerned with complaints about the way
things are being done, charges of mismanagement of
various kinds. The nearest they come to criticism of
basic Party policy is in an occasional carefully
phrased letter asking for clarification of certain matters of doctrine. Letters not printed are supposed to
be sent to persons in a position to act on them, and
the newspapers regularly report action taken on unpublished as well as on published letters, including

reprimand, dismissal, and sometimes even indictment of persons about whom complaints are received.

In a recent study of 270 such letters, drawn from eight different Soviet newspapers over a period of several months, Inkeles and Geiger found that complaints about the poor quality and unavailability of particular consumers' goods and of housing, and the unavailability and misuse of industrial equipment and other products, predominated. They found no mention of real deprivation of personal liberty or political freedom, or of the restrictions on labor or the burden of the norm system, though these are undoubtedly sources of real dissatisfaction. Evidently, either Soviet citizens do not dare to express these grievances or else the press refuses to publish them.

The complaints nevertheless cover a large area of everyday Soviet life. The roof leaks, and nothing is done about it. The stairway has collapsed and it is difficult for the writers to get to their second-floor apartment. A shopkeeper refused to hand over the store's "complaint book" to a dissatisfied customer. An aged and infirm doctor has not received his pension. Proper oil extraction machinery in Baku is

sadly lacking. Rarely is there mention of socialism
or Stalin or the Party or Marxism-Leninism or the
greatness of the Soviet Union — a fact which, as
Inkeles and Geiger point out, distinguishes them
from every other type of material published in the
Soviet press. The letters are concise and to the point;
for example:

I often have to use the dial telephone which is located
in the booth near the last stop of street car no. 27 (in
Koptev). It is out of order and works only in rare
instances. Who has any use for such a telephone?
(signed) A. LINSKY

In almost 90 per cent of the 270 letters there was
an explicit calling to account of at least one person,
group of persons, or organization for not carrying
out its job properly. "The modal pattern of accusation took approximately the following form: 'The
chairman of the district soviet, Comrade Ivanov,
knows about this situation but does nothing, and so
the situation remains the same.' " The targets of attack included ministries, soviets, trade unions, and
other social agencies, and in a very small percentage
of cases Party organizations — chiefly on the local

level, but also on the republican and all-union levels.

To what extent these letters are "planted" is an open question. What relation the published letters bear to the unpublished is another. The purpose of their publication from the point of view of the Party and the press, however, is clear: they are supposed to expose deficiencies in the operation and implementation of plans, policies, and principles dictated from above, and they are supposed to imply that by correction of those operational deficiencies the plans, policies, and principles can be made workable. From the point of view of the reader, however, they may carry different implications; and by pointing up the soft spots in the system they may have a long-range effect on the plans, policies, and principles themselves.

8

Religion in Soviet Russia

THE following letter appeared in *Komsomolskaia Pravda*, the newspaper of the Young Communist League of the U.S.S.R., on April 25, 1951:

DEAR EDITORS:

When an elderly man believes in God and performs religious rites, that is understandable: he received his education before the revolution; here we have survivals of the past and mere force of habit. We also see young people studying in ecclesiastical seminaries and explain this by their exceptional backwardness. But we have occasion to meet individual boys and girls who have grown up and been educated just like all our young people but who have religious prejudices and believe in some sort of "spirit," believe in "fate." Where do they get these beliefs?

We consider that to believe in God is to doubt science, to doubt one's own powers. Can our young

people really have any such doubts? And it is strange
to hear some people's assurances that religion does not
hinder communism. In our opinion this is political
shortsightedness. Is our reasoning correct?

MIKHAIL and ALEXANDER MARKOV, *Kiev*

The reply of the editors expresses the basic policy
toward religion which the Soviet government has
gradually worked out over the past fifteen years.
They write:

Your reasoning is quite correct, Comrade.

Religion cannot help hindering the building of communism, for it represents an antiscientific, reactionary
ideology. Religion gives a fantastic, false and perverted
idea of nature and society . . .

Why, then, ask some readers, do churches exist in
our society, why is not religious preaching prohibited? . . .

For the very reason that neither closing down the
churches nor prohibiting the performance of church
ceremonies are effective measures for combating religion . . .

The Party . . . combats religion by the only correct, ideological means — educational work, conviction,
elucidation, large-scale dissemination of political and
scientific knowledge. This work must be carried on
without offending the feelings of those who believe;

the reactionary and antiscientific essence of religious
ideas must be patiently and convincingly explained . . .

"Where do they get these beliefs?" ask Mikhail and
Alexander Markov in surprise. Our boys and girls do
not live their lives isolated from society, do they?
And inasmuch as society is not yet finally purged of
survivals, traditions and customs of the past which
have lived on in the minds of people, these viable,
tenacious survivals are in individual cases assimilated
by young people as well.

The advice to these and various others who have
written similar letters is, in substance: There is no
point in complaining that young people in your village go to church, or participate in religious marriages and christenings; the thing to do is to improve
the educational work of your Young Communist
clubs.

Why are the editors of *Komsomolskaia Pravda*
anxious not to offend the feelings of those who believe? The answer is twofold. In the first place, the
Soviet leaders have learned from hard experience
that religion thrives on such offenses. As the former
head of the now defunct League of Militant Atheists, Emil Yaroslavsky, himself once said: "Religion

is like a nail — the harder you hit it on the head, the deeper it goes into the wood." In 1937, after two decades of bitter struggle against religion, Yaroslavsky reported that two thirds of the adults in the villages and one third in the cities still believed in God.

In the second place, the Soviet leaders have apparently come to the conclusion that certain churches, particularly the Russian Orthodox Church, though representing "an antiscientific, reactionary ideology," nevertheless may — if properly controlled — serve Soviet social and political objectives.

In the 'twenties and 'thirties, the antagonism of the Bolsheviks to religion was manifested in the trial of church leaders as counterrevolutionaries, the closing of thousands of churches and monasteries, and the prohibition of all forms of church activity except religious worship. The latter prohibition was spelled out in a 1929 law which forbade church associations to give material aid to their members, to hold special meetings for children, youth, or women, to hold general meetings for religious study, recrea-

tion, or any similar purpose, to open libraries or
reading rooms, or to keep any books other than
those necessary for the performance of worship
services.

In 1929 a "Five-Year Plan for the elimination of
religion" was undertaken by the League of Militant
Atheists. Priests were caricatured in posters and
burned in effigy. In new cities like Magnitogorsk no
churches were built. A systematic and intense antireligious propaganda was carried on.

The first indication of a new policy of religious
tolerance was the enfranchisement of the clergy under the 1936 Constitution. (The widely hailed Constitutional guarantee of "freedom of religious worship and freedom of antireligious propaganda"
represented no change of the earlier law: religious
worship was still construed very narrowly and antireligious propaganda very broadly.) In 1937 wage
penalization for attendance at religious festivals was
discontinued. But the purges of 1937–1938 brought
renewed attacks on churchmen as spies and wreck-
ers, as well as heavy taxes resulting in the closing of
many churches that had survived to that time. At

the end of 1938 the pressure was visibly relaxed.

In 1939 State Art Workshops undertook the manufacture of religious articles. In 1940 the seven-day
week was restored, with Sunday ("Day of Resurrection") as a common day of rest. In 1941, a few
months after the German invasion, the publication
of antireligious journals was discontinued, the
League of Militant Atheists was dissolved, the antireligious museums were closed, and the heavy taxes
on church buildings lifted.

During the war the churches rendered invaluable
aid in maintaining the morale of the armed forces
and of the people. The Russian Orthodox Church
even raised 300 million rubles to help war production; it also gave special attention to the care of war
orphans. More important, the war itself was given
a religious character. A tank column was named
after Dmitri Donskoy, a fourteenth-century Russian
Orthodox saint. Alexander Nevsky, also a Russian
Orthodox saint, was glorified as one of the great
heroic models for the embattled Russian people.

Metropolitan Sergius, the Acting Patriarch since
1925, declared the defense of the Motherland to be

a sacred Christian duty and called Stalin "the divinely appointed leader of our military and cultural forces." Bishops and clergy who supported the Germans were excommunicated. The Church played a leading part in exposing and denouncing German atrocities, particularly the vandalism in the churches, and a leading ecclesiastic was named to the Extraordinary Commission for Investigating War Crimes — the first cleric to receive a Soviet appointment to a leading secular body.

Stalin repeatedly expressed his gratitude to the clergy for their part in the war effort. In 1942 he received the leaders of the Russian Orthodox Church and gave them permission to convoke a council of nineteen bishops who elected Sergius as their patriarch. In January 1945, after Sergius's death, a National Council of the Russian Church was convened in Moscow, attended by about forty bishops and also by clerical and lay delegates from the dioceses and by patriarchs and other representatives of eight non-Russian Eastern Churches. The new patriarch, Alexei, had previously acclaimed Stalin as "the wise leader placed by the Lord over our great country." In 1947 he was awarded The Order of The Red Banner.

In 1943 two theological academies were established for the training of priests. The publication of religious books was resumed. The establishment of new churches was undertaken with the aid of over one hundred local representatives of the Council of Russian Orthodox Affairs, a body created in October 1942 to act for the government in its relations with the Church. (In 1944 a separate council was established to represent the government in its relations with non-Orthodox groups.)

In August 1945, parishes, dioceses, and national churches were given the right to acquire, build or rent church buildings; local governing bodies were given the obligation to assist in repairing and improving church buildings; the tolling of church bells was permitted for the first time since the late 'twenties. In August 1946, monasteries were exempted from taxes on land and buildings.

In 1941, according to a Soviet report, there were 4225 Orthodox Churches, 8813 Orthodox clergy (including 28 bishops), and 38 Orthodox monasteries. Today it is estimated by foreign observers that there are about 29,000 Orthodox Churches, about 33,000 clergy (including more than 80 bishops), and about 90 monasteries and convents. The corresponding figures for 1917 are: 46,457, 67,210, and 1026.

A monthly religious periodical, the *Journal of the Moscow Patriarchate*, with a licensed circulation of 10,000 copies, carries articles on such subjects as church history, the liturgy, the lives of saints, questions of dogma, and like matters. The Church Calendar is circulated widely. Prayer books are printed. A few religious books, chiefly collections of articles and sermons, have been published since the end of the war.

The Church is financially independent, with large revenues derived from donations of the people. Taxes are very low. The government provides certain funds for the maintenance of some of the famous cathedrals and other buildings. High clerics are reported to have very large incomes and automobiles. The Patriarch resides in a palace in Moscow.

Since the end of the war, the teaching of atheism has again been stressed, but without the militancy of the earlier campaigns. The Society for Disseminating Political and Scientific Knowledge has replaced the League of Militant Atheists as the chief propagandist against religious belief. However, the Society is not a mass organization like the old League, which at one time had some six million members. It expressly seeks to avoid "arousing religious antagonisms."

The explanation of the new official policy of "ironic neutrality," as Trotsky called it, is not simple. A popular view is that the Soviet leaders are tolerant of religious belief because so few Russians are believers and those are mostly old people. While there are no statistics on the number of believers in Soviet Russia, American newspapermen have estimated that in Moscow at Easter crowds of 500,000 to a million have gathered around the overflowing churches. On other big holidays, too, the churches are more than filled, and Sunday attendance is also large. Yaroslavsky estimated in 1937 that over half the adult population were believers, and it is likely that the number is greater today, in the light of the resurgence of religious belief during the war.

Some observers state that many young people and children are to be found at church services. My own contacts with Soviet displaced persons in France and Germany during the war — not the so-called nonreturners, but those who were going home — confirm the impression of widespread religious belief among Soviet young people. A young woman told me, for example, that she had been the head of a Young Communist group and that she was also a believer. "All the propaganda against religion just went in one ear and out the other," she said.

Another theory is that the Communists were only interested in smashing the Church as an institution, and that now that the Church is no longer hostile or dangerous they have no reason to oppose it. It is true that there could have been no reconciliation with the Church if it had clung to its original position that the Bolshevik leaders were, in Patriarch Tikhon's words of 1918, "monsters of the human race." However, earlier Soviet policy was motivated less by anticlericalism than by atheism and the desire to replace "religious prejudices" by "scientific Marxism." Lenin said that he was more afraid of the good Christians who really believed, than of the hypocritical Christians who used religion as a cloak for material interests.

In addition, while the Church has paid many tributes to Stalin and to the Soviet social system, it has often reiterated its opposition to the atheism and materialism of Marxist doctrine. This is the one and only voice of public dissent from official doctrine which is permitted by the Soviet state. It is the one point of open cleavage between the six million Party members and sixteen million Young Communists who are forbidden to go to church, and large sections of the people. The Church is the only social organization in the Soviet Union in which the Party is not the "leading core." Its potential disruptive influence on the Party is evidenced by the fact that on occasion leaders have felt it necessary to remind Party members that they should not attend church, and the Soviet press has carried reports of Party members expelled for religious practices.

A clue to the explanation of Soviet religious policy may be found in the sharp discrimination in favor of the Russian Orthodox Church and the continued hostility toward certain other churches. The Roman Catholic Church is bitterly attacked for obvious reasons of international politics. Catholics in Moscow may attend the only Catholic church within the prewar boundaries of the Soviet Union; however, its connections with the Vatican have been virtually severed through the appointment by the Soviet government of a priest to serve Russian communicants, leaving the former priest to serve non-Russians, chiefly foreign diplomats. In the territories annexed from Poland in 1939, the three and a half million Catholics of the Eastern rite (Uniats) were in 1946 separated from Rome and incorporated into the Russian Orthodox Church, from which they had been separated since 1596; subsequently most of them were transferred to Poland, in an exchange of minority groups; the remaining Catholic bishops were arrested and many Uniat churches were delivered to the Orthodox groups. In the Lithuanian Soviet Republic, where the large majority of the people are Catholics, it is reported by Catholic sources that all or almost all the bishops have died, fled or have been deported.

Jewish religious life has also suffered some attacks, though not nearly so severe or systematic as those borne by Catholicism. While there is some evidence of official antisemitism, the denunciations of certain Jewish religious writings are expressly based on their pro-Zionist character. Zionism has always been considered by the Bolsheviks to be counterrevolutionary; today it is worse — it is unpatriotic and "cosmopolitan." The Yiddish press has been suppressed on the ground of "cosmopolitanism." However, those who are religious among the several million Russian Jews are not prevented from attending synagogue.

The fifteen to twenty million Soviet Moslems suffer in a still different way. Their religious worship is tolerated, and indeed since 1944 the resumption of pilgrimages to Mecca has been from time to time encouraged. On the other hand, Pan-Islamism has recently been under fire. Also certain social practices which are for many Moslems intimately connected with religion have been under continuous attack from the early days of the Soviet regime.

Polygamy, child marriage, and related customs are punished under a section of the criminal code dealing with "Survivals of Kinship Life."

Although there is no overt discrimination against Protestants, except possibly in the newer Soviet Republics of Estonia and Latvia (where the Lutherans constitute a vast majority of the population), there are no such favors meted out to them as are granted to the Russian Orthodox. The same is true of the Old Believers, a large dissenting group which split off from the Russian Orthodox Church centuries ago.

Strangely enough, the Baptists, with two to three million members, are treated especially well. There are some 3000 churches, organized in a Union of Baptists and Evangelical Christians. The Evangelicals include Adventists, Dukhobors, and Mennonites. A periodical, *Brotherly News,* is published by the Baptists. In 1946, visiting American Baptist ministers attended services and preached to large crowds of Russian Baptists. They said they found Russian Baptist worship "just like any service back here."

Of course, the Soviet state uses or abuses the various denominations for its own purposes. The Russian Orthodox Church is favored partly because it is willing to co-operate in the discrimination against certain other groups, such as the Roman Catholics. Also the Russian Church has for centuries accepted political subservience to the state, in the Byzantine tradition. Perhaps even more important is the fact that the Russian Church best represents both the Russian national and imperial heritage, which the Communists now seek to revive, and the Russian people, whose leading role in the Soviet empire of peoples the Communists now proclaim.

On the other hand, the Russian Orthodox Church uses the Soviet state for *its* own purposes. It is willing to pay a high price for the opportunity to train priests, publish religious literature, teach the young, conduct worship services — because it has confidence in the power of prayer. Russian Orthodoxy has always stressed the liturgy and common worship as against dogma on the one hand, or institutional organization on the other. As Paul Anderson has put it, in *People, Church and State in Modern Russia,*

"Stripped to the only elements permitted by law — conscience and celebration of the sacraments — the Russian Church makes bold to say that this is sufficient."

Whatever course the politics of uneasy compromise may take, the Russian people, both Marxists and Christians, will continue to be confronted with serious inner conflicts. In 1950 *Komsomolskaia Pravda* published a letter from a reader asking if Party principles permitted him to be married in a church ceremony, his fiancée being a believer and not a Young Communist. The answer, of course, was no. But the ultimate answer for Soviet Russia must depend, in part at least, on the relationship that is developed after the marriage ceremony.

9

Soviet Planning

IF Soviet experience is any guide, total planning, total centralization, simply does not work. The Russians believed in it, tried it, and had to abandon it.

It was the original idea of the Bolsheviks that under socialism the economy would be run by the State Planning Commission, a board of experts who would decide what was to be produced and how it was to be distributed and used. What has happened in fact, however, is that the State Planning Commission has been subordinated to the Council of Ministers, which has grown to include some forty economic ministries, each in charge of a particular branch of the economy.

Each of these ministries — such as the Ministry of Coal, Ministry of Automobiles, Ministry of Light

Industry, Ministry of Foreign Trade, Ministry of Finance, and so forth — has considerable independence. The State Planning Commission provides technical assistance — it integrates data — but it is the Council of Ministers and the individual ministries which issue the plans, and which are responsible for their fulfillment.

Moreover, within each ministry the various Chief Administrations and the individual factories and enterprises have been given a considerable degree of autonomy. Each state business enterprise operates on a profit-and-loss basis; it accounts for its own liabilities. Its profits provide large bonuses for managerial personnel and some benefits for workers. Important rights of possession, use and disposition of state property are exercised by the individual managers entrusted with operational responsibilities.

On the whole, the Soviets have moved in the past fifteen years toward greater decentralization of operations and toward increased personal incentives. Two illustrations of this movement may shed light on the general question of how a planned economy works.

First — contracts. While certain important and scarce materials are directly allocated, for the most part goods are transferred from one Soviet enterprise to another by means of contracts specifying the price, quality, time of delivery, and so forth. The terms of the contracts must be based upon plans and regulations; nevertheless there is very often considerable leeway for negotiation.

Hundreds of thousands of contract disputes between state business enterprises are litigated every year in a special system of courts, and although many of them turn on the interpretation of plans issued by higher authority, many others are adjudicated on orthodox principles of commercial law. Indeed, even where there has been a definite deviation from the plans, the contract may in some cases be controlling. Thus where a cartographical factory had ordered seventeen million pieces of tin stamp from a producers' trust but then refused to pay the price on the ground that its planned task had only called for eight million pieces, the court held that the defense was inadequate and ordered that the contract be performed as agreed. In another case a machine-construction plant sued a linen factory for the price of a machine, and the defendant joined its superior Chief Administration as a codefendant on the ground that the Chief Administration had promised to assign funds for the machine but had failed to do so; the court held that the fact that the Chief Administration had not been authorized by the state budget to assign funds for the machine, and that it did so through the irresponsible acts of its officials, did not release it from liability.

Other cases differ little from American commercial cases. The parties are government corporations, but their disputes rage over offer and acceptance, bills of lading, the insurer's claim to reimbursement from the carrier, the liability of agents acting beyond the scope of their authority, and many of the other matters that vex American businessmen and lawyers.

Why has contract, once condemned by Soviet leaders as a "bourgeois" institution destined to "wither away" under a planned economy, been restored as an essential part of the system? The an-

swer which the Soviet writers now give is illuminat-
ing: because, they say, "excessive regimentation"
(and that is their own term) freezes the flow of
commodities; and because "the state seeks to create
among the managers and workers of its establishments a direct interest in the results of their efforts."
The contract allocates responsibility and reward;
management's profits are an index of its success as
well as a source of personal income.

A second illustration of the compromises which
the Soviet economic system has made with the original conception of socialism, may be found in the
system of wages. The Soviet rulers are no longer
interested in equality of remuneration; indeed,
"equality-mongering," as Stalin has called it, is
denounced as a "left deviation." "To each according to his work" is the announced slogan of Soviet
socialism; and in fact inequalities of income are
probably at least as great in Russia as in the United
States.

Now, if everyone is not to be paid equally, the
problem of central control of wages becomes very
difficult. The central authorities can, of course, and

do enact certain rates, certain norms. They can and do provide for wide variations, in different localities and industries. But suppose two workers operate drill presses in the same plant, and one machine is old and decrepit while the other is new and efficient. On a piece-rate system, one worker will be very unhappy unless some allowance is made for the condition of the machines.

Because such situations are numerous, the Soviets allow for adjustments to be made by the individual managements of enterprises on the basis of special conditions. These adjustments are authorized in so-called "notes" to the norms. For example, in ditch digging the norm for filling a ditch is about 12 cubic meters in eight hours. But by use of the notes relating to whether the soil is sandy, stony, rocky, whether it is level or on a slope, and the like, the norm can be reduced to about 3 cubic meters. Because labor is scarce, there is a strong tendency to apply the notes liberally, and it appears that in many types of work the notes have in fact replaced the norms.

As a result, enterprises consistently everexpend

the wage fund assigned to them. In the first Five-Year Plan of 1928, it was planned that the average annual wage per worker in 1932 would be 994 rubles; actually in 1932 the average annual wage was 1427 rubles. The planned annual wage for 1937, under the second Five-Year Plan, was 1755 rubles; the actual 1937 average wage was 3047 rubles. This phenomenon has recurred regularly although production plans have in general been underfulfilled. It is not hard to imagine the enormous inflationary effect it has had on prices, taxes, and costs, and the difficulties it has created for the planners.

Examples could be multiplied to show that centralized planning is in itself no solution to basic economic problems. The planners must face the same fundamental economic realities that exist in a non-socialist society. Indeed the complexities are overwhelming. The point is, however, that the bottlenecks have caused a re-emphasis of managerial responsibility and initiative, strong personal incentives both of reward and punishment, "business accountability," decentralization of operations. With this the old ghosts return.

Apart from the efficiency of the Soviet economic system — Does it work? — there is the moral and legal question, Is it just? Soviet economic planning has endangered the system of justice by producing a vast increase in criminal offenses. Certain standards of economic behavior are required by law. Not merely the contract between the parties, but the law itself, is violated by the manufacture or sale of goods of poor quality, by waste of money or property, by malicious refusal to comply with the terms of a contract, by "abuse of authority" or "negligent attitude to duty" by a manager or other economic official. The dockets of the regular Soviet courts are crowded with cases of these economic and official crimes, including absenteeism and quitting by workers.

This extension of criminal law has been accompanied by a greatly increased emphasis on the subjective factor of intent. Departing from their original theory that a criminal intent is not a prerequisite for guilt, and that the courts should simply examine the social danger of the act committed and of the individual himself, the Soviet courts now stress (except in certain cases) "the subjective side" — the individual's state of mind when he committed the act, his desire or foresight of the consequences and, in many cases, his purpose or even motivation.

For example, the official in the tin-stamp case mentioned above, who contracted to purchase more than the plans for his enterprise authorized, would be guilty of "abuse of authority" only if he knew or should have known (and in imputing such knowledge a subjective standard would be applied: not whether any "reasonable man" but whether the particular accused man personally should have known) that the act was illegal. Under Soviet Supreme Court decisions he would be guilty of malicious breach of contract only if he directly intended to cause harm to the state.

The accent on knowledge and intent would seem to be related to the economic system. The plans and regulations require legal sanctions; on the other hand, they tend to reflect economic objectives, goals which often cannot be met 100 per cent. If all deviations were punished indiscriminately there would be chaos. It is the "grossly negligent" or "malicious" deviator who is considered dangerous to the system.

To prove or disprove the grossness or wrongful purpose of an act of mismanagement is in general very difficult. In many cases it comes down to the question of the accused's character or his loyalty; personalities and politics may replace strict standards of legality in determining the outcome. Central control of the economy thus tends to endanger the objectivity of law.

Even more serious, perhaps, is the pressure which the system exerts upon managers and other officials to commit these economic and official crimes. Since plans are not 100 per cent effective, since there are bound to be weak links in the chain of production and distribution, the manager is apt to find himself in a position where he cannot fulfill his planned tasks without going outside the authorized channels of procurement or supply, or without in some other way violating the law. Shall he maliciously fail to produce the required quota of automobiles, for example, simply because some supplier has failed to send him the carburetors; or shall he deliberately produce automobiles "of poor quality" (also a crime); or shall he procure carburetors by illegally swapping some items which he has (illegally) hoarded? His best alternative, probably, is the third — but if something goes wrong with the automobiles, he may find the deal exposed and himself in a labor camp.

A former Soviet lawyer, who was general counsel of the Odessa Bread Trust from 1931 to 1941 and who is now in this country, tells the following story:

The Odessa State Confectionery Plant lacked nails to fasten together the crates in which it shipped confectioneries to all parts of the U.S.S.R. Generally the plant manufactured its own nails from wire, but on this occasion it could not procure the wire. As a result the plant's warehouses were full of unpacked products and they had to be stored outside. The manager had no right to stop production, since that would have meant non-fulfillment of the plan. The plant worked twenty-four hours a day, in three shifts, but the time came when even tarpaulins were lacking, to cover the perishable goods lying under the open sky.

The manager therefore sent his procurement agent to Moscow to see if he could obtain wire. The agent succeeded in procuring 800,000 rubles' worth from the Academy of Sciences. Permission was obtained from the Ukrainian branch of the State Bank to transfer the necessary credit from the Confectionery Plant's account. The wire was bought and shipped to Odessa; nails were made from it, the crates were fastened, and the perishable goods were saved from spoilage and delivered to the customers of the Confectionery Plant under its various contracts.

Three months later it was learned that the wire, unbeknownst to the procurement agent, had previously been stolen from the Moscow subway, then under construction. In tracking down the stolen wire, the police uncovered the crime of the illegal procurement of wire (a so-called "funded" product which may only be transferred with proper authorization of superior administrative organs). A criminal prosecution was brought against the manager and the procurement agent for "abuse of authority," and against the treasurer of the plant for "neglect of official duties." The manager was sentenced to three years' deprivation of freedom in an agricultural colony, the procurement agent to ten years in a corrective labor camp; the treasurer was fined 25 per cent of his pay each month for a year.

In spite of severe penalties, illegal economic activities are highly organized in Soviet Russia. "Pushers" represent managers in supply depots to see that materials are expedited. Swapping and borrowing is common. Bribery and black-market operations are carried on very widely — not only by congenital lawbreakers but by respectable managers who seek thereby to fulfill their planned tasks. There are also other strains on morality, if not legality. The matter of influence, "pull" — in Russian, *blat* — used, for example, to get priorities; the Russians say privately that *blat* is even higher than Stalin. There is "dirtying one's eyeglasses" (*ochkovteratel'stvo*): one overfulfills the plan for making skis by making children's skis. There is "looking the other way": the enterprise overstates its needs to the Chief Administration, and the Chief Administration overstates its needs to the ministry, and so on up the line.

There is a third question to be asked of an economic system — in addition to Does it work? and Is it just? — the question of freedom. To what extent does it permit freedom of personal movement, freedom of political expression, freedom to think and say and do the "wrong" things. Such freedoms are severely limited in Soviet Russia, but that is not due exclusively to the economic system. The Soviets started with political and intellectual absolutism. They have run economic, political, and intellectual controls in triple harness — a Russian troika — from the beginning.

It is important to note what the Soviet system offers its people instead of freedom. It offers them discipline, service, sacrifice, authority, unity. To Americans these military virtues perhaps do not have much appeal. We should not underestimate, however, the potency of their appeal to Russians, with their craving for a sense of social unity and purpose. Even in America a call to duty and to service may, in a period of crisis, find a greater response in the minds and hearts of men than a reassertion of individual rights and freedoms.

While some may espouse the cause of centralized planning as a scientific solution to economic problems, its real attraction is its social militancy, which lifts people above their individual pursuits and mobilizes them for service to society. Soviet planning has had from the start the character of a military campaign. The plan is accomplished by "assaults on economic fortresses"; "communiqués" are received from various "fronts"; "shock brigades" are used to "storm bastions"; medals are awarded to Heroes of Socialist Labor.

From the standpoint of economic development, this spirit is effective for accomplishing the big and spectacular tasks, such as building huge hydroelectric projects, steel mills, and the like. It is effective for moving large numbers of people. But even in other less conspicuous forms of activity, the emphasis upon service to society, upon the country's needs rather than the individual's needs, may give satisfaction and meaning to lives otherwise frustrated and demoralized.

It is the reaction against social anarchy, the urge to unity, which makes dictatorship possible. But by a strange paradox, dictatorship tends to destroy the very unity upon which it is founded. By terrorism, secret-police activities, denunciations, the totalitarian regime tends to split society asunder, to scare men back into their private corners, to atomize them. People of different walks of life do not converse freely; each stays in his little circle. Thus specialization returns to undermine a unity which is artificial because it is unfree. How far this tendency has gone in Soviet Russia is one of the underlying themes of this book.

10

Soviet Law in Action

JUDGING from the narratives of former political prisoners in Soviet labor camps and from reports of the various treason trials in Russia and other Communist countries, one gains an impression of the goddess of Soviet justice with the blindfold removed and the scales weighted heavily in favor of the political interests of the rulers. Of what significance is law and justice when behind the legislators, administrators, and judges stand the Communist Party and the secret police?

It seems naïve, however, to suppose that strict legality on the one hand, and impartial justice on the other, play no role whatsoever in the daily functioning of Soviet society. How could a planned economy operate with any degree of effectiveness without not merely regulations but also some objective standards for their interpretation and enforcement? How could a social order have any degree of stability or command any support from its members unless there existed some impartial forum for the adjudication of disputes and some outlet for the feelings of justice which exist in all people?

These are not answers, but questions — questions intended to suggest the complexity of what Soviet jargon calls "the situation on the legal front." This suggests another well-known phrase, non-Soviet, generally used in a different sense: "the struggle for law." Law — as strict legality and as impartial justice — exists in the Soviet Union, but its existence is precarious. It must be defended against assaults from many sides. From certain areas, notably that of political opposition, it is excluded almost entirely. In other areas, notably that of disputes between private individuals over rights of property or contract or liability for personal injury, law occupies most of the battlefield. In still other areas the forces are more evenly matched.

The coexistence, side by side, of a system of

force and a system of law has raised the question to what extent the system of law is merely a paper system, in books, and to what extent it is real and applicable in action. To this question the scholars have been able to give no definitive answer, for the simple reason that without direct access to the Soviet Union, without free observation of Soviet conditions and free discussion with Soviet citizens, there can be no definitive answer. We are somewhat in the position of those who study the Roman law of the time of Justinian. We can describe the Soviet legal system in some detail, but we can only discuss in general terms its significance in the daily life of the people. Even illustrations drawn from reported cases in the Soviet Supreme Court, or from cases in the lower courts noted in Soviet legal periodicals, leave open the question whether they are typical or aberrational.

Unlike the students of the old Roman law, however, we do have access to a few living persons who have in the recent past practiced law in the Soviet Union. Among such persons is one who was

a professor of law in Odessa from 1925 to 1944,
and who also served from 1931 to 1941 as chief legal
adviser of a large Soviet state business enterprise,
the Odessa Bread Trust, which had some eighteen
subordinate plants and enterprises. Evacuated from
Odessa by the Germans in 1944, and liberated by
the Americans in 1945, Professor Boris Konstantinovsky and his wife and two daughters decided
to seek asylum in the United States — because of
their antipathy to Communism as a political system
and because of their fear of persecution if they
returned to Russia.

Professor Konstantinovsky has recollected and
reported his legal experiences in Soviet Russia, including over one hundred court cases with which
he was connected. These cases were mostly concerned with the problems of the Odessa Bread
Trust, arising from commercial disputes with pur-
chasers or suppliers, from labor relations, from in-
terrelations with superior and subordinate enterprises, and from the many other troubles that beset
a large business unit. Some cases involved criminal

prosecutions in which Professor Konstantinovsky represented the accused or which he merely observed.

The present chapter is built around a few of the cases reported by Professor Konstantinovsky — those that seem best to illustrate the extent to which Soviet law is merely a paper system and the extent to which it is an active force in the lives of Soviet people. Of course these cases are only "some evidence" of general Soviet practices; conflicting examples could undoubtedly be found. But they are representative of the experience of someone who was there — and they are interesting.

The first, the case of Rusakov, is an example of the abuse of the judicial process by a Communist Party organ for political purposes — and of the cautious but effective opposition to such abuse by several persons, including the judge and the regional procurator. The case does not tell how often opposition is raised to such abuse, how often it is effective, or how often the abuse itself is attempted. Professor Konstantinovsky states that this is the only case in his personal experience of direct interference by a Communist Party organ in the conduct of a trial.

1. *The Case of Rusakov*

In 1940, during the Russo-Finnish war, Odessa faced great provisioning difficulties, especially with regard to the supply of bread. All bread shops were besieged from morning to night by long queues. At this critical moment, the highest organ of government in the Odessa region — the Regional Executive Committee — decided, in accordance with an order of the Regional Committee of the Communist Party, to find a scapegoat for the hitch in bread supply and thus slough off responsibility for bad administration.

Such a victim appeared in the person of an employee of the Odessa Bread Trust, Z. Rusakov, who was in charge of writing out orders for the supply of bread to state trading organizations. Among his duties was the writing of orders for "spoiled" bread to be used as fodder for horses of the State Transport Co-operative. These orders Rusakov wrote by authorization of the Regional Trade Division, the highest regional institution for the regulation of internal trade. The spoiled bread was sold at a price established by the People's Commissariat of Food of the U.S.S.R. — that is to say, at fifty kopecks per kilogram. In all of 1940, the State Transport Co-operative received not more than two tons. The population of the city — over 600,000 people — consumed from 225 to 240 tons of bread daily.

Criminal proceedings were instituted against Rusakov on the ground that in supplying spoiled bread for horse fodder, rather than for sale to the population via trading organizations, he had created a crisis in the city, a crime under Article 97 of the Criminal Code (abuse of authority). The absurdity of this accusation was more than obvious. An investigation was nevertheless completed, and Rusakov brought to trial.

Two days before the court was scheduled to meet — in a demonstration trial at the club of the bakers' union — the judge conducting the trial came to see the director of the trust and held a private

conference with him. The judge, point-blank, asked
the director, as an influential member of the Communist Party, to help him. The judge said that he
himself was convinced of Rusakov's complete innocence, but that he had an order from the Mu-
nicipal Party Committee to sentence Rusakov to
five years' deprivation of liberty. This meant, actually, exile to a labor camp, since deprivation of
liberty for over three years was served in labor
camps. The judge, realizing that he would have to
decide the case contrary to the dictates of his conscience, and sentence an innocent person, asked the
director of the trust to do everything in his power
to save Rusakov. The director of the trust, fully
realizing that Rusakov was simply a scapegoat for
the sins of others, and that nothing could be hoped
for from the trial, invited the chief legal adviser
[namely, Konstantinovsky], the chairman of the
local factory committee, and the secretary of the
party organization of the trust, to his office for a
consultation. It was decided to contact the regional
procurator and to try once again to have the case
discontinued. With great difficulty, these people

managed to get an appointment with the procurator, and they persuaded him to put an end to this
scandal. As a result of this consultation, the mu-
nicipal procurator who was prosecuting the case
against Rusakov was directed to consent to a motion for postponement of the case and for a new
investigation. The judge and Rusakov's attorney
were informed of this decision.

The next day the judge, in the presence of the
assembled bakery workers (about one thousand
men), granted a motion by the defense to postpone
the hearing of the case and to order a new investigation with the consent of the procurator.

The next month the war with Germany began:
in July, 1941, all files of the Odessa courts and of
the procuracy were burned.

Rusakov, his innocence acknowledged by the
judge, the procurator, and public opinion, remained
at liberty.

In the second case, there is a different kind of
Communist Party influence suggested. In a civil suit
for 8000 rubles back salary, the defendant appar-

ently uses his prominent position in the Party to win his appeal from an adverse decision in the trial court. Again, however, there is resort to still higher governmental authority — in this instance higher judicial authority, through an appeal to the Ukrainian Supreme Court — and higher governmental authority is ostensibly not bound by the machinations of the lower Party organs.

A key figure in both the first and the second cases is the procurator. Indeed, the office of the procuracy is the key to the entire Soviet legal system. It not only prosecutes crimes but supervises the entire judicial and administrative systems. The procurators perform their functions independently of local organs and are subordinate solely to the Procurator General of the U.S.S.R. The regional procurator watches over the system of administration within the region and sees to it that regional executive and administrative bodies do not overstep their legal authority. He has the right to "protest" any act which in his opinion violates the existing law, to the executive-administrative office immediately superior to the body responsible for the

alleged violation. With regard to the judicial system, he not only acts as public prosecutor but also
watches all civil proceedings within his jurisdiction
and may initiate or enter any lawsuit at any stage
on either side; he also may appeal, or "protest," any
decision, civil or criminal, of any court of the region; he may move to reopen any case after a decision has been handed down. The procuracy main-
tains a special section to which anyone may address
a letter or telegram if he thinks an official injustice
has been done.

2. *Bant vs. the Odessa Regional Office of Grain Supply*

Bant, an official of one of the Odessa branches
of the People's Commissariat of Supply of the
U.S.S.R., had been commissioned by the chairman
of the Odessa Regional Office of Grain Supply
(*Zagotzerno*) to carry out a very complex and responsible operation, which involved directing the
transshipment of cargoes of grain arriving at the
port of Odessa and addressed to the Odessa Re-

gional Office of Grain Supply. Bant agreed to do
the job, which took about eight months. He carried out the assignment brilliantly and the grain
reached its destination. Instead of paying an hon-
orarium for his services, however, the chairman of
the Regional Office issued a directive in which he
expressed his thanks to Bant, explaining that, since
Bant worked in the same building in which the
Regional Office of Grain Supply was located, and
since his office and that of Grain Supply were both
subject to the jurisdiction of the same institution,
the Committee of Procurement of the U.S.S.R.,
Bant had been obligated to carry out the assignment without remuneration. Bant did not agree,
and brought a claim in the Odessa People's Court
for 8000 rubles against the Odessa Regional Office
of Grain Supply.*

The legal adviser of Grain Supply understood
very well how justified Bant's claim was, and refused to plead the case in court. Instead, the chair-

* Bant applied for aid to the legal division of the Odessa
Regional Council of Trade Unions, whose chief legal adviser
entrusted the case to Professor Konstantinovsky.

man of the Regional Office himself appeared in court. The court decided in favor of Bant. The Regional Office of Grain Supply appealed the case to the Odessa Regional Court. On appeal, there appeared to be no doubt that Bant had a legal right to remuneration and, from the remarks of the judges and the procurator, it seemed quite clear to all present that the appeal of Grain Supply would be quashed. It is therefore impossible to describe the amazement of Bant's lawyer when, appearing three days later at the office of the regional court, he learned that the decision of the people's court had been reversed and Bant's claim rejected.

Bant suspected strongly that the chairman of Grain Supply, a quite important member of the Communist Party in the city, had approached the Regional Committee of the Communist Party and that the members of the regional court had been influenced to pronounce a decision against their own persuasion — since their views to the contrary had been clearly expressed during the argument on appeal.

This suspicion was increased when some days

later the chairman of Grain Supply called a conference of his administrative employees at which he condemned the lawyers of the Regional Council of Trade Unions who had supported the "self-seeking" demands of Bant, and added: "It is true I am not a trained lawyer, but I got what I wanted; my own chief legal adviser and Konstantinovsky, who supported the grabber, lost the case and once again Soviet justice came out on top."

It was then decided to approach the procurator of the Ukrainian Soviet Socialist Republic with a request to have the case sent to him for protest before the Ukrainian Supreme Court.* This the Ukrainian procurator consented to do, and the civil division of the supreme court set aside the decision of the regional court, giving judgment for Bant. However, the president of the Ukrainian Supreme Court did not agree with this decision and protested

* Normally, the losing party is permitted one appeal as of right, but at the protest of the procurator, in his "supervisory" function, the case may be brought for review in the supreme court of the particular republic and ultimately by the Supreme Court of the U.S.S.R. Likewise the president of the supreme court may protest a decision for review by the full bench of his court.

it to the full bench (Plenum) of the Ukrainian Supreme Court, which in turn did not agree with the
protest of its president and left the decision of the
supreme court in force — that is, decided the case
finally in favor of Bant.

The following three cases illustrate a still different sort of threat to strict legality and impartial
justice, in which the straight political element is
mixed with an ideological element. Mrs. Imertsaki
loses the first (though not the last) round of her
struggle because her deceased husband had been
a White officer. Misha Dresher is initially convicted of "swindling" because he not only concealed his "bourgeois" class origin upon applying
for admission to the university, but also continued
to have "ties with his parents" after his admission;
ultimately he is acquitted on the basis of a change
of policy. A judge fears lest too many acquittals
may lead "them" to complain that "his class vigilance has weakened," but he is persuaded by counsel that his duty to follow the law comes first.

3. The Case of Mrs. Imertsaki

Mrs. Imertsaki, a middle-aged widow, worked as bookkeeper in the technical training division of the Odessa Bread Trust. With her daughter, a schoolgirl, she occupied one room of a two-room flat. It was necessary to go through her room in order to reach the second room, in which there lived a Communist Party worker of some authority, who attempted systematically and by every means to force Mrs. Imertsaki to move out of the room she occupied. With this object in mind, he behaved in such a way as to create conditions quite impossible for joint habitation of the flat.

Mrs. Imertsaki asked the local trade-union committee of the technical training division to help her by setting up a lacquered partition in her room, since the other inhabitant, not in the least concerned that the lady and her young daughter lived there, took the liberty of bringing women from the streets up to his room at night. The union local readily agreed to help by financing the setting up of a partition. The other lodger, however, would not permit the partition to be set up. The regional committee of the bakers' union requested the chief legal adviser of the trust to help Mrs. Imertsaki and to bring suit in court in order to obtain a legal resolution of this dispute. Meanwhile, the situation in the communal flat had become so unbearable that on the eve of the trial Mrs. Imertsaki attempted to commit suicide.

The people's court granted Mrs. Imertsaki's petition. There followed on the part of the lodger in question an appeal to the regional court, which reversed the decision of the people's court and dismissed the case, referring in its decision, among other things, to the fact that Mrs. Imertsaki had been the wife of a White officer. The procuracy refused to protest this decision to the supreme court.

Encouraged by the regional court's decision, the lodger released his inhibitions still further and began to molest Mrs. Imertsaki's daughter. It was quite impossible to find even the smallest coop of a room elsewhere, and Mrs. Imertsaki had to go on living under the onerous conditions of the transit room. There followed another attempt at suicide.

Strange as it may seem, the Yezhov purge of 1938 helped set the matter straight. At about this time practically the entire staffs of both the Odessa Regional Court and the Odessa Regional Procuracy were purged as "enemies of the people." (Some committed suicide, as, for example, the regional procurator Turin, who, when he was summoned by the NKVD, hanged himself in the lavatory of the procuracy.)

A new opportunity was thus presented to petition the regional procuracy to aid this unfortunate woman. Now the procuracy readily agreed and protested the case to the supreme court. Among other things, it appeared that the records of the case had disappeared completely from the court's archives. On the basis of a ruling of the Ukrainian Supreme Court, Mrs. Imertsaki was permitted to bring suit all over again in the people's court and, in both instances (in the people's and regional courts), her claim was now satisfied.

4. *The Case of Misha Dresher*

In 1934, a year before the university reforms which canceled a whole set of restrictions on those entering higher educational institutions ("Children need not answer for the sins of their fathers. . . ."), Misha Dresher, upon entering the Odessa State University, failed to reveal in his application that his father had been a tradesman. Instead he stated falsely that he had been a shop assistant. Two years later, when Dresher was studying in the third form, the secretary of the District Committee of Komsomols exposed him before the rector of the university, revealing his real origin and describing him, incidentally, as a "class enemy" who during the civil war, had come out against the Red Army and had even busied himself with speculation, though actually the youth in question was no more than five years old during the civil war in the Ukraine. On the basis of this information, Dresher was excluded from the university and a criminal case of false pretenses ("swindling") was invoked against him, under Article 169 of the Criminal Code.

At the trial in the Odessa People's Court the
accused pointed out that he had long since liberated
himself from any financial dependence on his father,
that he had washed away the "shame" of his origin
by active participation in social service ever since
his school days, that he had now broken with that
milieu into which it was hardly his fault to have
been born. But the people's court, turning a deaf
ear to all the protestations of the accused, found him
guilty, since there was at hand a simple and easy
opportunity to tag him as an "alien element" and
apply the "fashionable" Article 169. The court took
as a ground for its decision the fact that he had
"ties with his parents" (by "ties" was apparently
meant the fact that on occasion he permitted himself
to write letters to his mother). He was sentenced
to compulsory labor tasks — that is, a monthly de-
duction from income — for a period of six months.
On appeal, the conviction was affirmed by the regional court.

The case was then brought before the Supreme
Court of the Ukrainian Soviet Republic, on protest
of the chief justice of that court. The supreme

court handed down the following decision: As is apparent from the facts of the case, Dresher actually did conceal his social origin; but this did not provide grounds in the given concrete instance for bringing him to trial for false pretenses under Article 169 of the Criminal Code, because his aim had been, after all, to study, and not to derive material gain. The reason for restricting persons of non-proletarian origin from entering higher institutions of learning is to prepare cadres of specialists from working-class youth or those of working-class origin. Dresher had participated in the Young Communist movement, had been a correspondent of Pioneer and Komsomol newspapers, had led social work, and had labored from his early youth. He is, essentially, a toiler, and the fact that he happened to be born into the family of a small trades-man provides grounds neither for his conviction nor for his exclusion from the university where he had been studying for some time. Formally, there is, of course, this deed — the fact that he included false information in an official report made to a state institution. This would support administrative action by the university authorities. The statement that he had ties with his parents is supported only by the fact that he corresponded occasionally with his mother, but no indication of material support from his parents has been established.

On the basis of these considerations, the supreme court reversed the judgment of the people's court and the regional court and dismissed the case, but admonished Dresher.

5. A class-conscious judge

The cashier of the Third Odessa Bakery, Mr. Shargorodskii, was sent by the management to collect the payroll of 11,000 rubles from the local office of the State Bank. He received the correct sum at the bank, packed it into his portfolio, and took the trolley back to his place of work. On the way, in the overcrowded car, some malefactors who apparently had been following him and knew that he had received a large sum of money at the bank slashed his portfolio with a razor, took out part of the money, and vanished. When the cashier arrived at the bakery, he noticed the loss of nearly 6000 rubles. He informed the treasurer that the money was missing.

The plant manager informed the procuracy of all that had happened, and the procuracy brought charges against Shargorodskii, accusing him of negligence in his official duties under Article 99 of the Ukrainian Criminal Code, as a result of which the state had been damaged to the extent of some 6000 rubles.

When the director of the trust heard of the charges against Shargorodskii, he arranged legal aid for him, taking into account that the cashier had worked in the bread industry for many years, that he enjoyed full confidence, and that he had been an active trade unionist. The trade-union representatives shared the point of view of the manager. Therefore, by order of the manager, the chief legal adviser of the trust was to act as defense counsel in court, for which purpose he was given special authorization by the trade union.

The Shargorodskii case was the fourth to be heard at that session of the people's court. In the first three cases, the court had pronounced acquittals. In defense of Shargorodskii, it was argued to the court that the loss incurred by the plant ought to be borne by the administration of the plant because it had failed to provide Shargorodskii with means of transportation to get the money from the bank to the plant. Instead, the administration of the plant had permitted Shargorodskii to use the trolley for this purpose, where the risk of theft, one might say, was more than likely. Moreover, Shargorodskii had repeatedly requested Mr. Dolgo-sheienko, the plant manager, to provide him with the management's car to pick up the money. All this was confirmed by witnesses, among others the plant manager himself. Indeed, the considerations pointed out by the defense were so convincing that an acquittal seemed certain to all attending the session.

Before retiring with the people's assessors for consultation, however, the judge said to the defense counsel:

"Comrade legal adviser, how can I acquit this man when I've already acquitted three before him?

You know, they won't pat me on the head for that. They'll say, 'He's pooped; his class vigilance has weakened.' . . . I, too, have a 'plan.' "

So the legal adviser of the trust had to point out to the judge that his duty was to decide the case according to conscience and not according to "plan."

After a prolonged conference the court handed down an acquittal with a separate opinion appended by the judge. The protest of the procuracy against this acquittal was quashed by the Odessa Regional Court.

The concluding case of this chapter shows the summary removal of a judge in direct violation of the provisions of the 1938 Judiciary Act. The case illustrates the paradoxical position of a government seeking to enforce by illegal means the "stability of laws" which Stalin in a famous 1936 speech said "we need now more than ever."

6. The removal of a lenient judge

By an edict of June 26, 1940, workers and employees were made criminally responsible for being late more than twenty minutes and for unwarranted absence from their jobs. The law, still in force, provides that lateness over twenty minutes is to be punished by not more than a fine of 25 per cent of the worker's or employee's pay each month for six months ("compulsory labor tasks at his place of work"). A supplementary directive made it obligatory for all judicial organs of the U.S.S.R. to impose the *maximum* penalty provided for in the edict.

Soon after the edict had been issued, the people's judge of one of the workers' districts of Odessa, Mrs. Morozova, in trying a criminal case involving charges against an Odessa factory worker who had been more than twenty minutes late to work, took a number of circumstances into consideration and pronounced an acquittal.

The district procuracy protested the decision to the Odessa Regional Court, which reversed it, and sentenced the accused worker to the maximum penalty provided for by the edict of June 26.

At the order of the Communist Party, Mrs. Morozova was promptly removed from her job for "not being able to cope with her work" and "for failing to maintain constant vigilance" — despite the provision of the Judiciary Act that judges may be removed from office only by recall of their constituency or upon criminal conviction by a court.

Less planned, less rehearsed, less "staged" than many official Soviet activities, judicial trials of ordinary criminal and civil cases (as contrasted with major political trials) effectively dramatize the real relationships between the people and the state. From these unofficial reports, as even from many of the officially or semiofficially reported cases, one gains an impression that there are bold litigants and courageous judges and procurators in Soviet Russia, who carry on the struggle for law against the forces of arbitrariness in the Communist Party and in the system itself.

At the same time, these cases — and the hundreds of thousands of others litigated in the overcrowded dockets of Soviet courts each year — illustrate the fact that a dictatorship depends both upon legality and upon the desire for justice: upon legality in order to formulate and effectuate its policies, upon justice in order to make people believe in those policies. But true belief cannot flourish without freedom to disbelieve. In its fear of disbelief, the Stalinist regime is apt to panic; threatened by some real or imagined discontent, it may throw law and justice overboard and go back to its basic reliance upon force. This is the struggle within the system itself; the struggle between the need for stability and the revolutionary spirit. Soviet law in books reflects the need for stability; Soviet law in action reflects the struggle.

||

The Communist Party of the Soviet Union

"THE Communist Party of Russia," wrote Edward Crankshaw in 1947, "has been compared to a religious order, but usually in terms of a metaphor or an analogy. There should be no metaphor or analogy about it. It *is* a religious order. . . ."

Hear the words of the Party rules of 1939:

The Party is a united militant organization bound together by a conscious discipline which is equally binding on all its members. The Party is strong because of its solidarity, unity of will and unity of action, which are incompatible with any deviation from its program and rules, with any violation of Party discipline, with factional groupings, or with double-dealing. The Party purges its ranks of persons who violate its program, rules or discipline.

It is the duty of a Party member: (a) to work untiringly to improve his political knowledge and to master the principles of Marxism-Leninism; (b) strictly to observe Party discipline, to take an active part in the political life of the country, and to put into practice the policy of the Party and the decisions of its bodies; (c) to set an example in his observance of work discipline and state discipline, to master the technique of his work and constantly to improve his industrial or economic qualifications; (d) constantly to strengthen the ties with the masses, promptly to respond to the needs and demands of the toiling people, and to explain to the masses the policy and decisions of the Party.

The Communist Party of the Soviet Union is not a political party in the Western sense. It represents no class, no special political-interest group or groups; for though the 1939 rules called it "the organized vanguard of the working class," its membership was even then drawn largely from the "toiling intelligentsia" — that is, the managerial, professional, and white-collar classes. It does not campaign against any other party in Russia, for there is no other party. The Party is rather the "central core of conscious socialists," the "shock troops" in all phases of social, economic, and political life.

The religion of this new "communion of saints" is Marxism-Leninism as reinterpreted by Stalin. Lenin was the apostle to the gentiles who adapted the Marxian gospel to a new generation and a new people. Marx and Engels — building on German philosophy, French political science, English economics — developed a science of society in the Western tradition. Their theory of historical materialism was a "scientific" explanation of the rise and fall of classes, with emphasis on economic determinism and the inevitable overthrow of the capitalist order by the revolutionary proletariat. Lenin — building on the Russian revolutionary tradition — seized on a different side of Marxism: its messianism, its faith in the ultimate triumph of "consciousness," reason, over the material conditions of existence. It was Lenin who founded the Communist Party as a disciplined conspiratorial elite of superconscious revolutionaries who would lead the "unconscious masses" to power and then, in time, would transform the proletarian dictatorship into a classless socialist society.

If Lenin is the St. Paul of Marxism, Stalin is the

Soviet Emperor Constantine, who has made of the new religion a state orthodoxy. Stalin has purged the Party of the revolutionary romantics, the men who were in love with revolutionary ideas. He has subordinated reason to loyalty. The Party has become a professional priesthood of officials, administrators, technicians, and privileged workers. The ideas have become dogmatized and stereotyped, a liturgy to be memorized and chanted.

While continuing to exalt the person of Lenin, Stalin has greatly modified the Leninist concept of socialism. The Soviet state and the Communist Party are called Leninist, but they have almost entirely lost their Leninist character — except in the sense that if Lenin had lived he, too, might have felt compelled by events to alter his original ideas. A striking witness to the change is the new set of Party rules adopted in October 1952 at the Nineteenth Party Congress, the first to be held since 1939. The new rules drop the phrase "organized vanguard of the working class"; instead the Party is defined as "a voluntary militant union of single-minded Communists, organized from people of the working class, the toiling peasantry, and the toiling intelligentsia." Marxism-Leninism is mentioned rather incidentally as the fifth of a new list of eleven duties of Party members: the member is enjoined "to work on the development of his own consciousness, on the acquisition of the fundamentals of Marxism-Leninism."

The 1952 rules also drop the "(b)," standing for Bolskevik, which formerly always came after the letters C.P.S.U. (Communist Party of the Soviet Union). "Bolshevik," meaning literally majority-er, was the name given in 1903 to the Leninist half of the old Russian Social Democratic Labor Party; its elimination by the Nineteenth Party Congress was officially justified on the ground it was "unnecessary." However, the name "Bolshevik" was a symbol of the revolutionary zeal of the Party. But long before 1952 Stalin had eliminated practically all the leading "Old Bolsheviks" who had made the Revolution. By 1939, hardly any of the original leaders were left; of the two-and-a-half million members only 8 per cent had joined before 1920, and 70 per cent had joined after 1929 or later.

About 91 per cent of the higher leadership and about 92 per cent of the secretaries of lower party organizations were under forty years of age. The 1939 rules removed the difficulties that had previously been placed in the way of nonworkers who sought to join; the "party maximum," restricting the income which members could receive, had been abolished many years earlier.

Between 1939 and 1945 the number of Party members increased to about 5,800,000; by September 1947 it had reached 6,300,000, of whom some two thirds had joined during and after the war. In October 1952 there were 6,884,000 members. During the war there were some cases of whole units enrolling. Ideological requirements were greatly relaxed. Although the rate of new admissions to the Party has fallen off since 1947, and there has been a tightening up of Party discipline, nevertheless it is apparent that the rank and file of today are not like the zealots of the 'twenties and early 'thirties — before the great purges of 1936 to 1938. The new 1952 rules accept that fact. The emphasis on duties is increased;

the role of beliefs is diminished. The Party retains
the discipline of a religious order, but the religion
has been watered down.

The basic unit of the Party is the so-called primary party organ, consisting of three or more members. These "cells," as they were once called, are
established in factories, offices, state farms, collective farms, army and navy units, schools, and so
forth. They take an active part in trade union and
other meetings; their main job is to "agitate and
organize among the masses," to strengthen labor discipline, to expose deficiencies of all kinds.

The primary Party organ does not have — as it
did in the early 'thirties — a direct voice in the
management of a business enterprise or other organization; the 1939 and 1952 Party rules give it
the right to "control" management activities, but
by control is meant only a general supervision. It
is given the right to put questions to management,
and to make recommendations. As a matter of practice the director of a business enterprise, almost in-
variably a Party member himself, will often consult with the secretary of the Party unit of the

enterprise, but management is primarily his own responsibility. Similarly on collective farms or in government offices, the primary Party organ plays an important secondary role as critic and agitator but is not supposed to make the day-to-day decisions.

The primary Party organ is itself governed by an annually elected bureau of not more than six members, or, if it has less than fifteen members all together, by a secretary. If there are less than 100 in the primary Party organ, the members of the governing bureau are not excused from their regular work in order to carry out Party duties.

Over the primary organs stand the city and district committee of the Party, elected by annual conference of delegates from the primary organs, but subject to confirmation from above. (A 1938 Party decree requires that the first, second, and third secretaries of all city and district committees be confirmed by the Central Committee itself, in Moscow!) The city and district committees consist of full-time paid Party officials, whose job is to keep an eye on economic and political affairs at the city and district levels, and to see that the primary Party organs under them function properly. They are separate from the local governing bodies, though their members may be strategically placed in the city councils and other top local executive agencies.

Over the city and district committees stand the regional, territorial, and republican Party committees, corresponding to successively larger political-administrative divisions of the country. The agenda of a meeting of a regional committee might consist of discussion of the preparation for sowing and harvesting, the extent of fulfillment of plans for livestock breeding in collective farms of the region, the work of city and district committees in accepting new Party members, deficiencies in the work of the press or of the judiciary, or any of a hundred other matters affecting the region.

At the top of the hierarchy stands the Central Committee of the C.P.S.U., in form elected by and responsible to the Party Congress. In fact the Congress is a rubber stamp for the Central Committee. Under the 1939 rules it was supposed to convene

every three years; the 1952 rules have changed it
to four; but since 1925 it has actually met at intervals first of two, then of three, then of four,
then of five, and then of thirteen years. The 1952
Congress comprised 1359 delegates. The Central
Committee, with 125 members, performs on a national scale the job done locally by the local committees. One or more of its members may be particularly responsible for the coal industry, another
for agriculture, another for the press, another for
the nationalities problem, and so on.

Theoretically the Central Committee elects the
Political Bureau (Politburo) and Organizational
Bureau (Orgburo) — combined under the 1952
Party rules into a Presidium — and the Secretariat.
Again, in practice, the chain of command has run
the other way. Headed by Stalin, the Presidium,
with twenty-five members and eleven alternate
members, in fact has complete control over the
Central Committee, just as the Central Committee
has complete control over the republican Party
committees, the republican over the territorial, the
territorial over the regional, the regional over the

city, the city over the district, and the district over the primary Party organs. The setup is pyramidal, and as the rules state, "The decisions of higher bodies are absolutely binding upon lower ones." Similarly the theoretical accountability of each of the executive bodies to a conference or congress of delegates from subordinate primary Party organs is contradicted by the factual superiority of the executive bodies. Likewise, within an executive body the authority in fact descends from the secretary. "Bolsheviks are centralists by conviction," stated the author of a 1945 Soviet textbook on administrative law.

Stalin himself likened the Party structure to that of an army, when he said in 1937 that there were three groups within the Party: a "General Staff" of about 3000 to 4000 members, an "officers' corps" of about 30,000 to 40,000, and 100,000 to 150,000 "noncommissioned officers." Altogether these groups made up less than 10 per cent of the membership at that time.

However, the leadership principle does not necessarily render the lot of the leader an enviable one.

There is a heavy turnover of Party leaders both at the local level and higher. Chiefly they are removed on the ground of inefficiency in rooting out shortcomings of the organizations and areas which they are supervising. If a factory fails to fulfill its production plan, the blame may fall not only on the manager but also on the primary Party organ, the city Party committee, the regional Party committee, and so on up the line; and, on the other hand, Party agencies which go too far in attempting to root out shortcomings, by trying to take over the functions of economic or political administration, are also subject to criticism on that score.

Removal of Party leaders for inefficiency often results in their transfer to other responsible jobs — at least so the press complains. Expulsion from the Party is a different matter. In the mass purges of the late 'thirties hundreds of thousands of Party members were not only expelled but sent to labor camps with or without trial. These mass expulsions were exceptional, and have not been repeated in Russia. The 1939 and 1952 rules state that when the question of expulsion arises "the maximum caution and comradely consideration must be exercised." Since 1939 many members have been expelled as "not qualified," and many have been put on probation. The new Party rules introduce the provision that a member who commits a crime considered punishable by the courts shall be expelled.

The new Party rules also centralize control over Party discipline in the hands of a new Party Control Committee whose representatives are independent of local authority. It has been thought by some that this presages new mass purges. However, there is little other evidence for this view. In general, since 1939 the pressure on Party members has been considerably relaxed. Although there have been serious breaks in Party line since the end of the war, and many leaders have been attacked for deviations, public "confessions of error" have in almost all cases sufficed to keep unity. In holding the Party together greater reliance can now be placed on incentives of power, prestige, and material well-being that go with high administrative positions in management, government, the army, the secret police, the professions, and so forth — positions un-attainable without Party membership.

The Party stands behind the Soviet state, using state agencies to accomplish its objectives.* But it is Stalin's Party — the Presidium's (late Politburo's) Party — and Stalin is the head of the state as well. He is chairman of the Council of Ministers which runs the daily affairs of the state; also many members of the Presidium occupy official government positions. Stalin and his circle of advisers use the Party apparatus to accomplish the objectives of the state. State and Party interpenetrate.

Thus from the standpoint of power, the relation between Party members and the other 97 per cent of the people is one of rulers and ruled. This simple relation is complicated by the fact that the Soviet regime does not want the Russian people merely to obey; it wants them also to believe in the rightness of the orders they are given. As someone has said, Stalin seeks to make the people want

* The new Party rules state that the Party committee at territorial, regional, and republic levels shall "guide the activities" of the corresponding governmental and public organs "through the Party groups within them."

to do what they have to do. Indeed, there are many
indications that the regime is acutely aware that in
the long run, at least, it cannot stand without the
support of its subjects. Many times (though not always) it has shifted policy because of popular resistance. Thus the Party is conceived as another
"transmission belt" between the state and the people, designed to mobilize mass support for Stalinist
policies and also to feel out and report areas of popular discontent.

In a formal and external sense, the transmission
belt works. At national elections, for example, the
Party succeeds in getting some 99 per cent of the
voters to register their support for the single slate of
candidates and the single platform. But the very size
of the vote testifies to the pressures that are used.
The Party is feared; is it respected?

I asked two émigré Russians, man and wife,
whether they thought Party members in general
were sincere believers or merely careerists. The
man, who had been an economist in the Ministry of
Light Industry of one of the smaller republics, answered: 95 per cent of them are cynics, who are in

the Party solely for the privileges it brings. The wife said: That is not true — I would say that 95 per cent of them are misguided idealists and true believers in Marxism. I asked them if they could tell me about any particular Party members whom they had known socially. The answer was — neither of them had known any socially.

Party members are a fraternity which the 97 per cent see, for the most part, only from the sidelines. There is little informal give-and-take, little friendship, between Party members and non-Party people. They rarely meet except for business or official reasons. If of two brothers one joins the Party they are very likely to drift apart.

Nonfraternization, apparently an unwritten rule of the Party elite, symbolizes the regime's disillusionment regarding any genuine conversion of the masses of Soviet people to a belief in Marxism-Leninism. This disillusionment has undoubtedly contributed to the Party's own loss of faith in the doctrines of the founding fathers of socialism, and the consequent replacement of many of those doctrines by the old-fashioned virtues of patriotism, self-sacrifice, discipline, unity. Of course, there is still the Party line — in biology, in linguistics, in history, in foreign policy, in everything: Party members must follow its devious course without themselves deviating. But the official doctrine is the servant of the elite, rather than the elite the servant of the doctrine. The official doctrine is the badge of unity. The regime seems to agree with the statement, attributed to the Englishman Melbourne, that it doesn't matter what we say as long as we all say the same thing. What people really think, however — not the official line but the working beliefs — is something else again: that does matter, but it is not openly discussed.

"The Party," wrote Lenin in 1917, "must be teacher, guide and leader." In the past fifteen to twenty years, in the name of stability, the Party has taught or permitted the strengthening of social institutions and traditions which, in an inner sense, challenge its own position — institutions and traditions, such as the family, one-man management, the army, law, the Russian Orthodox Church. In the absence of political parties, or for that matter of any real freedom of public opposition, inner conflicts are concealed under terms such as the new "socialist" family, the "socialist" ruble, "socialist" military discipline, "socialist" legality. Only with respect to the Church, which explicitly differs with the Party on at least one fundamental question, does the conflict come out in the open: one cannot by any stretch of Marxist terminology talk about the new "socialist" church.

These traditional elements of stability do not threaten the external political strength of the Party — which continually tightens its control over them — but its inner position as "teacher, guide and leader." They foster independent loyalties.

The Russian Revolution of November 1917 is not over, and its course is no doubt as unpredictable as ever. Yet the guess, at least, may be hazarded that the Communist Party of the Soviet Union — "Bolshevik" no longer — will continue to lose in inner cohesiveness and in the coherence of its doctrine as it continues to maintain the external discipline of its members and its external control over the Soviet social order.

12
The Discipline of Terror

TERROR, the threat of physical violence, is not merely a temporary excrescence of the Bolshevik seizure and consolidation of power, as it was once fashionable to think, but an essential part of the Soviet system. This does not mean, however, as some have assumed, that every Soviet citizen has his suitcase packed in anticipation of being whisked off to a labor camp in the middle of the night.

There are two kinds of Soviet terror, distinguished both by their causes and their consequences. One is mass terror, which has recurred periodically in Soviet history, striking wildly at certain large and loosely defined groups. The most recent examples are the postwar "liquidation" of certain peoples — the Crimean Tatars, the Chechen and Ingush in the

North Caucasus, and the Ossetians — who were considered untrustworthy because of their collaboration with the German invaders; apparently with little or no attempt to weed out innocent from guilty, the regime simply scattered these peoples to various parts of the Soviet Union. Also, in amalgamating the Baltic peoples of Latvia, Lithuania, and Estonia into the Soviet Union, the regime has removed large masses of people who, on the basis of social background or occupation, are considered insufficiently loyal to their new Motherland. During the war, an estimated one-and-one-half million Poles were sent to Soviet labor camps — often without even a pretense of trial — not because they had done anything but because the Soviet regime considered them a problem.

Apart from these instances of terror directed at whole peoples or classes, the latest appearance of mass terror within Soviet Russia occurred during the late 'thirties. The notorious purges of 1936 to 1938 were directed chiefly against members of the Communist Party, though many others fell by the wayside. The occasion was Stalin's well-founded fear of secret opposition within the Party. By the time the fury of his revenge had spent itself, it was impossible to tell why any particular person was chosen to be a victim. Total Party membership decreased from over three-and-one-half million to less than two million between 1933 and 1938. As Zhdanov himself told the Eighteenth Party Congress in 1939, first the counterrevolutionaries were purged, then the purgers were purged, and then the purgers of the purgers. The report of Zhdanov's speech, in which he gave absurd examples of expulsions from the Party and urged the abolition of mass purges, indicates "laughter" at many points — a macabre suggestion of the relief that must have been felt by his audience. Actually, even before this speech, Beriya, having taken over the People's Commissariat of Internal Affairs (NKVD) from the traitor Yezhov (who had previously replaced the wrecker Yagoda), had ordered the release of many thousands of prisoners condemned falsely and in many cases without formal charges having been brought against them.

Prior to the outbreak of the purges of the late

'thirties, mass terror had been invoked in the early 'thirties against the opponents of collectivization — chiefly the kulaks or well-to-do peasants, officially numbered at almost six million in 1928. How many hundreds of thousands were sent to labor camps, deported to remote regions, or killed in that period is not known. The "liquidation of the kulaks as a class," as it was officially called, was the first use of mass terror since the initial period of the Revolution, when Lenin established the Cheka (Extraordinary Commission for Fighting Counterrevolution, Sabotage, and Crimes by Officials). From December 1917 through 1920 the Cheka waged what Lenin himself called "the Red terror"; persons considered hostile to the new regime, after a secret informal administrative trial, were shot, sent to concentration camps, or deprived of their property, not because it was proved that they had done something but because terror was considered an important means of maintaining the Bolsheviks in power. As Latsis, one of its leaders, wrote in 1921: "In its activities, the Cheka has endeavored to produce such an impression on the people that the mere mention of the name Cheka would destroy the desire to sabotage, to extort, and to plot."

Apart from these successive waves of mass terror, each directed at a somewhat different "problem" and therefore endangering the lives of somewhat different groups of people, there is a second kind of Soviet terror, an individualized terror, which is directed against anyone who by word or deed brings upon himself suspicion of disloyalty to the regime. This terror is designed not to solve any particular problem but to keep each individual in line, to prevent deviations from the Party orthodoxy. To this second kind of terror, but not to the first kind, Maynard's statement is applicable: "The Terror has been tolerated, because it has not touched the masses. When, and if, it touches them the regime will be in danger." It is just because the regime is already in danger that mass terror is invoked. Individualized terror, on the other hand, is directed against a danger to the regime which is far less immediate. It chiefly touches individual persons who occupy positions of some responsibility — Party officials, business managers, professors, high army officers, and so

forth. Individualized terror has existed throughout
Soviet history, and has been especially rampant in
times of mass terror; in the early 'thirties, for example, many of the "right deviationists" who had op-
posed the program of rapid industrialization and
collectivization found themselves in labor camps
alongside the kulaks.

The chief mechanisms of Soviet terror are the
Ministry of Internal Affairs (MVD) and the Ministry of State Security (MGB). These organizations
are direct descendants of the Cheka, which in 1922
was reorganized as the State Political Administration (GPU – renamed Federal State Political Administration, or OGPU, in 1923), which in turn was
transformed into the People's Commissariat of
Internal Affairs (NKVD) in 1934. Within the
NKVD there was created a Chief Administration of
State Security, which was eventually made a People's Commissariat of State Security (NKGB); all
People's Commissariats were renamed ministries in
1946.

The Ministry of Internal Affairs has been called
"a state within a state." It has its own armed forces,

which guard the frontiers as well as factories, bridges, and buildings which have military importance. It has its own "judicial" system for the trial of political enemies. The regular police force and fire department are under its jurisdiction. It is in charge of important highways. It is in charge of the Bureau of Vital Statistics and of the internal passport system. It runs the corrective labor camps and other penal institutions.

The "judicial" powers of the Ministry of Internal Affairs are exercised by a "Special Board," which has the right, under a 1934 statute, to sentence "persons suspected of being socially dangerous" to a labor camp for a period up to five years or to banish them to a particular locality for a period up to five years. The board consists of the Minister of the Interior or his representative, certain heads of departments of the ministry, the procurator of the ministry, and others; persons who have been tried by it state that it contains thirteen to fifteen members as a rule. Its procedure is informal; it is bound by no rules. Defense counsel is generally not permitted, and in many cases the accused has been tried in ab-

sentia. Even the provision limiting the power to sentence may easily be circumvented by prolonging the
period of detention prior to sentencing or by simply
passing a new five-year sentence upon expiration of
the old. During the mass purges, people were often
sent to labor camps first and sentenced by the Special Board later.

The Special Board is entirely separate from the
regular judicial system for the trial of nonpolitical
criminal and civil offenses, as well as from the system of military courts which tries not only crimes
committed by servicemen but also certain crimes
against the state, notably treason, no matter by
whom committed. The MVD investigators may decide to turn the case over to the regular courts or to
the military courts. The major purge trials of 1937
and 1938 of Zinoviev, Bukharin, Radek, and other
"Trotskyites" were judged by a military tribunal,
the Military College of the Supreme Court of the
U.S.S.R. These were "demonstration trials," and
were exceptional — designed to give a legal gloss to
the extralegal actions of the Special Board.

A case which the MVD ultimately turned over to

the regular courts is recounted by one who later
fled, Dmitri Buligin. Buligin, who has described his
experiences to me personally in great detail, was a
professor of engineering in Leningrad. In 1940 he
drew up plans for an important construction project
in Kazan. Unfortunately for him, the foundations
sagged. He was immediately summoned by the
NKVD and charged with a "deliberate act of sabotage," designed "to prevent the new plant from getting into the production of our country's needed
war potential." Because he was doing important
work he was not detained during the preliminary investigation, but was severely questioned many times.
His chief assistant was kept in detention, however:
"He's a rather suspicious character," the investigator told Buligin. "His father was a priest, and he
has relatives abroad. In the Engineering Institute he
did not have a good record, either. He didn't participate in any of the social work. Did you know
him well?"

Buligin says that he was terrified of the question-
ing, until one day the investigator charged him with
belonging to a group which was plotting the resto-

ration of the Tsardom. This struck Buligin as so pre-
posterous that he suddenly relaxed, realizing that the
investigator was simply spinning charges out of his
head.

After two months Buligin, his chief assistant, an
engineer who had been working on the construction project, and a foreman, were indicted — not for
counterrevolutionary sabotage, which would almost
certainly have meant trial and conviction by the
Special Board, but for criminal negligence. They
were tried by a regular Moscow court, convicted,
and sent to labor camps — but subsequently on appeal to the Supreme Court of the RSFSR, the conviction was reversed and they were released.

If it is asked whether this experience is "typical,"
the answer is that it is impossible to know. There are
countless stories, certainly, of persons whom the
MVD did not turn over to the regular courts for
trial. Buligin states that when he was in the hands
of the MVD he felt little or no hope of escaping a
harsh sentence, but that once he was turned over to
the regular courts he was confident that he would
be able to prove his innocence and that he would be

acquitted. The line between terror and legality is apparently well understood; but it is the MVD which decides on which side of the line a particular case falls.

Because Buligin was an engineer he was sent to a labor camp which was engaged in the construction of a large industrial plant, where he was given a responsible job with better pay and more privileges than other prisoners. In the short time that he was there he saw no unusual occurrences to break the monotony of a barracks life of hard work and confinement.

Was Buligin's labor camp experience "typical"? Again, it is hard to generalize. The number, location, and types of labor camps, and the number and types of persons serving in them, are closely guarded secrets of a very small group of Soviet leaders. From many independent reports of former inmates, we know that the camps vary a good deal — from railway and canal camps of the far north to sheep farms in Central Asia, from construction camps near Moscow to lumber camps or gold mines in Siberia. Sentence to some camps is generally considered by

Soviet citizens to be "a prolonged death sentence." Within a camp, conditions are in general much worse for political prisoners than for ordinary criminals.

Various estimates have been made of the number of prisoners; three-and-one-half million (Jasny), five to seven million (Prokopovich), seven to twelve million (Dallin), ten to fifteen million (Atkinson), and on up to twenty million (Kravchenko), and over. These estimates are based on analysis of Soviet population and production statistics, budgets of the MVD, eye-witness reports of particular camps by former prisoners, and other sources. Until the Kremlin attempts, at least, effectively to refute the estimates made abroad it cannot blame the rest of the world for suspecting the worst.

One argument against a high estimate of the labor-camp population is that, judging from all reports, women constitute a small percentage of the prisoners — probably less than 10 per cent — so that a camp population of, say, ten million would mean the withdrawal from normal life of over 20 per cent of the adult male population, even apart from the armed forces. There is little evidence of so great a dearth of men in the cities and villages. Furthermore, slave labor requires a large number of guards and supervisers, perhaps one for every 20 prisoners, and in any case is notoriously inefficient for all but a few purposes; to rely on it as heavily as the higher estimates suggest would mean that the Soviet regime is either more insecure or more stupid than we have reason to believe.

Imprisonment in a labor camp is the usual sentence for all crimes punishable by deprivation of freedom for more than three years. Some more important convicts are sent to prisons of the more conventional type. A sentence of three years or less is generally served in an agricultural or labor colony, where a good deal more freedom is allowed. The Special Board of the MVD may also impose the penalty of banishment to a particular locality. Mrs. Nora Murray, a Soviet woman who married an Englishman and received Stalin's permission to leave Russia in 1942, states that her father, a high Party official and associate of Litvinov in the Ministry of Foreign Affairs, was sentenced in 1939 to ten years'

205 of terror 205

imprisonment by the Military College of the Supreme Court of the U.S.S.R. — a victim of the Nazi-
Soviet pact. Her mother was sentenced to five years'
administrative exile in Kazakhstan in Central Asia,
without the right to live in a town. She wrote to
her daughter that after terrible hardships she found
a home with some Asiatics who let her live with
them, doing odd jobs like cleaning out their pigsties,
and that eventually she found a menial job as char-
woman in a nearby labor camp.

Of the Ministry of State Security — the MGB —
little is known, within the Soviet Union or without.
Apparently the MGB has taken over from the
MVD primary responsibility for counterintelligence
— in the broad Soviet sense, which includes detection of hostile tendencies in the population. Informers report to it any signs of disaffection. The MGB
and MVD work very closely together — they are
both headed by the same man, Lavrenti Beriya —
but the term Secret Police now refers primarily to
the agents of the MGB.

Of the work of the MGB in the army something
has been said in the chapter on the Soviet soldier.

The MGB's Special Sections exist also in the factories. How little the average Soviet citizen knows of what the Special Section actually does may be illustrated by the report of Boris A. Konstantinovsky, who was the chief legal adviser of a large trust. He states that there were Special Sections in the individual subordinate enterprises as well as in the trust itself. The office of the Special Section was separated from the rest of the premises by a door lined with a soundproof material and reinforced with lead, equipped like the vault of a bank. To enter the office of the Special Section was prohibited to all employees except the director of the trust or the manager of the particular plant, who could enter only by permission of the chief of the Special Section. All correspondence to the Special Section was delivered by a special courier to the director or manager personally, under the impress of five wax seals, and the director or manager was required to deliver it personally to the chief of the Special Section.

"What sort of functions did the Special Section have? No one, with the exception of specially entrusted persons, knows exactly. Judging by the fact

that the Special Section collected the military registration cards of the workers and employees, and
supervised fulfillment of military obligations and assignments to the armed forces, one may conclude
that the Special Sections were particularly responsible for military obligations. But this certainly is not
the fundamental role of the MGB in a Soviet enterprise. One must suppose that supervision of the
work and of the personal behavior, both at work
and outside, of each and every worker and employee, regardless of his party position, entered into
the round of the Special Section's duties. In any
case, in one respect the chief of the Special Section has more authority than the director himself,
for in the matter of delivering its correspondence
the director plays the role of a simple messenger
boy."

How do the Russians feel about these instruments
of terror, designed to strike fear — the fear of separation from home and family, of bodily harm, of
hard labor, of hunger, of death — into the hearts of
all potential opponents of the Soviet regime? The
question answers itself: they fear them.

But why does the Soviet regime resort to measures which alienate so many who might otherwise be its friends, both at home and abroad? There are many answers — psychological, sociological, ideological, historical, economic. One of the most important is this: with the prohibition of genuine political opposition and free public debate, there is no other effective method for discovering opponents than by secret police, and no other effective method of dealing with them than by physical removal. Any person who thinks against the Party line is a potential conspirator — for where else can his secret anti-Party thoughts take him but to secret anti-Party talk and then to secret anti-Party action? As Latsis wrote of the Cheka in 1921, the endeavor is to produce such an impression that the mere mention of the name MVD or MGB will destroy the *desire* to sabotage and to plot. That is "the discipline of terror," as Maynard has called it. For this reason I believe that though, given increasing social and economic stability, mass terror might finally disappear, individualized terror is an inherent part of the Soviet system.

The terror is explained by the system; the system is not explained by the terror. It has been the purpose of this series of sketches to put the terror in the focus of the system as a whole, and to trace some effects of the whole upon the daily lives of Russian people.